In a Sea of Wind

In a Sea of Wind

Images of the Prairies

Yva Momatiuk and John Eastcott·Camden House

CAMDEN
•HOUSE•
✿✿✿✿✿
PUBLISHING © Copyright 1991 by Yva Momatiuk and John Eastcott

Canadian Cataloguing in Publication Data

Momatiuk, Yva, 1940-
    In a sea of wind: images of the Prairies

ISBN 0-921820-39-9 (bound)
ISBN 0-921820-35-6 (pbk.)

1. Prairie Provinces - Description and travel - 1981-
-Views.*
2. Prairie Provinces—Social life and customs.
I. Eastcott, John, 1952-   . II. Title.

FC3234.2.M6   1991   971.2'03'0222   C91-094359-1
F1060.92.M6   1991

Front Cover: Freshly harvested grainfields, the Wintering Hills, Alberta

Trade distribution by
Firefly Books
250 Sparks Avenue
Willowdale, Ontario
Canada M2H 2S4

Printed and bound in Canada by
D.W. Friesen & Sons Ltd.
Altona, Manitoba, for
Camden House Publishing
(a division of Telemedia Publishing Inc.)
7 Queen Victoria Road
Camden East, Ontario
K0K 1J0

Designed by
Linda J. Menyes

Colour separations by
Hadwen Graphics Limited
Ottawa, Ontario

Printed on acid-free paper

Dogs working cattle, Ravenscrag, Saskatchewan

To Mek and Pecia, who nurtured

Power lines traverse the grain fields near Vulcan, Alberta

Acknowledgments

Gathering the material for this book took us from the torch-dry prairie summer of 1988 to the ice-crackling winter and the lengthening days of spring of 1989. During that year, many doors and many more lives were opened to us, and for this trust and generous help, we are profoundly grateful.

We are particularly thankful to Helga and Steven Hawczuk, Jars Balan, Carol and Jim Armit, Heather and Roger Beierbach, Vicky and Krzysztof Gephard, Edith and Dave Landy, Nancy and Grant Kyle, Christine and Allan Brown, Andrzej Olkowski and Angela Pedley, Baiba and Pat Morrow, Mike and Geraldine Wortas, Nina Shewchuk and Linda and Arnold Elliott, who sheltered, fed and supported us.

We are also indebted to those who told us about their present and their past, their hopes and disappointments, their aspirations and hard lessons, and who taught us so much while asking nothing in return. We thank Julie Cochrane, Evelyn Swain and the late Mary Bone, Paul and Fred Antrobus, Kenneth Brown, Heather Redfern, Linda Boudreau, Herbert Bouillet, Howard Buchanan, Gilles Danis, Randy Hayward, Dean Francis, Ralph Hedlin, Violet Kasper, Sophia Kaczor, Fred Sigmundson, Arlene and Alfred Dahl, Robert Wrigley, Marion Staff, Betty and Adolf Schlichting, the Sira family, Irka and Bill Balan, Wim Aberson, Margareth and Leo Mol, Susan and Raymond Kenny, Marjorie and Robert Robinson, Norman Tuplin, Lawrence Zurbyk, Gloria May and Ian McPhadden, Laura and the late Graham Parsonage, Stuart Houston, Joanne and Gordon Moulton, Philippe Mailhot, Joe Fafard, the Friesen family, the Wright family, Lawrence Beckie, Maria and Dominick Krupnik, Bonnie and Eldon Wurban, Ted Byfield, Ann and Allan Blakeney, Betsy and John Bury, Byrna Barclay, Gilbert Abraham, Jack Pye, Hugh Dempsey, Mary Ambroz, Marvin Schmalzbauer, Albert Johnson, Margaret and Willard Dow, Eric Wells, Kay Vaydik and Wayne Zelmer.

We are grateful to the Gross family of Pincher Creek Hutterian Brethren Colony and the Sunrise and Crystal Spring colonies, whose members shared their daily bread and knowledge with us; also to Christa Shirky and her family, who introduced us to the Hutterian way of life; and to the Cypress Hills Stockmen's Association members for their hospitality during their annual fall roundup.

Our thanks go to Richard Henry, Clifford Arnell and sons, Runa Aranson, Eve and John Beierbach, the Cheung family, Byron Crabb, Norm Czibere, Dale Friesen, Karen Gussie, Bob Gallup, Myra Laramee, the Norek family, Renie Gross, Shirley Hill, John Kushnir, Solange Liang, Kelly Leavesley, Robert Lyons, Jars Lozowczuk, Ria Lemstra, Gladys and Elmer Laird, Jack Langille, Barney Kutz, Wayne Lynch, Donald Mackenzie, Bill McDowell, John Margitich, Allan Murdoch, Robert Nero, Joyce Meyer, the Olson family, Pearl Ogryzlo, Emmie and Langford Oddie, Steven Prystupa, Ruth Purdy, Gloria Romaniuk, Gary Rempel, Paul Rupcich, Dave Scheller, Don Starkell, Francis Switzer, Burt and Joyce Strandberg, Alex Scalplock, Soren Tergesen, Orysia Tracz, the Walper family, Terry Mobberley, Nadya Kostyshyn Bailey, Mitch Podolek, Bruce Waddell, Gary Lawson, Johnny Sandison, Andre Lalonde, Ted Fontaine, Gilbert Comeault, Ed Mayer, Lyn Johnston, George Davies, Wasyl Makarenko, Keith Dryden, Radomir Bilash, Merna Summers, the Stacheruk family, Marc Chabot, Stan Cuthand, David Eberth, Beverly and Marcel Deschenes, Paul Banzet, Jau-nan and Byron MacLellan, Barbara Sapergia and Geoffrey Ursell, Bob Elian, L.H. "Scoop" Lowry, Halyna Freeland, John and Barry Graham, Louise Big Plume and Quinton Pipesteam.

We are grateful to Lisa Schneller, who painstakingly transcribed nearly 200 hours of prairie conversations, and to Gerald Miller, who helped clarify matters. Our thanks also to the staff of Camden House for making this book possible: director of books Michael Worek, art director Linda Menyes, graphic artist Roberta Voteary, editorial coordinator Lois Casselman, copy editor Christine Kulyk and associates Catherine DeLury, Laura Elston and Mary Patton.

Finally, we would like to offer our most heartfelt thanks to our daughter Tara, who once more explored and learned with us.

Yva Momatiuk and John Eastcott

The prairies came to us while we were on our way to somewhere else. Driving north through Alberta's wheat fields, we followed the curve of the Earth, heading for the Arctic to work on our first assignment for *National Geographic* magazine. The clouds raced overhead, but at noon, the wind dropped, and the desert-blue sky closed hotly upon us. Hundreds of miles later, exhausted, we came upon a tidy row of grain elevators, towering sentinels in the horizontal flatness of the prairie that cast cool shadows on the heat-flattened grasses. We hunkered down for the night close to their warm, grain-filled trunks. Then, during the coolest hours of darkness, a storm rumbled in from the Rockies and shook us awake. We watched lightning bolts dancing in the fields till dawn.

Since then, other images of the prairies have emerged: a row of combines in a plume of dust, a black bear disappearing into a thicket, a hawk suspended in that enormous sky. One day, we used to say, we would slow right down and take a good look.

And suddenly, we were there again, in the furnace of June heat hovering over the blinking ponds and sucking them dry. In southern Saskatchewan, farmers knelt in the furrows to check the shrivelled plants and rolled their eyes in sweaty surprise: it was like nothing they had known for a long time. They heard it was 106 degrees in Regina and there was some terrible, tornado-bound spell in Alberta. ''At least,'' they said, reminding us how lucky they were, ''we are still green.'' In the continent's parched, waterless midst, they shared all farmers' hope for better days.

This time, we moved slowly, stayed throughout the summer, well into the fall and again through the late winter and the thaw of spring. We listened to the voices of people in cities and in small

Royal Winnipeg Ballet

Ukrainian Catholic Church of the Holy Ghost, Sandy Lake, Manitoba

prairie towns scattered among the folds of this rich but often trying land. They spoke of hardship and hope, of daily bread and blood kin, of prejudice and tolerance, of resignation and defiance. They painted images of mirth and sorrow, for although life in the prairies is never carefree, it is always replete with meaning.

The only constant was the bond between the people and their land, and they carried it gladly, as if those ties did not restrain, but nourished them. Later, while editing the tapes of our conversations, we at times abbreviated and clarified the accounts but left intact the ideas, the thoughts and the passion. The words of the people of the prairies are the backbone of this book.

Yva Momatiuk and John Eastcott

A cowboy's horse

I feel like part of my horse, and he feels like part of me. That's the way it should be: you're one. He is your own legs underneath, and you can go where you want to go. He'll keep you warm when it's cold; and you can move him over here, and he enjoys it; and you can move him over there, and he enjoys that. You can handle him just by shifting your body.

He loves to have you there, and you love to be around him 'cause he can do all these things you couldn't do on your own two feet. He's essential to your life, and there's no way you can run a ranch without him. They can talk about all the motorbikes in the world, but they just ain't right. You can't look at your cow off a motorbike 'cause you can't get close to her, but you can do anything on horseback: a horse and a cow go together.

There's only one or two great horses you get in a lifetime, and you can never erase them from your mind. You'd like one like them again, but they don't come easy, and some horses you just don't get along with. It ain't that they're wild; they can be gentle as a pup and kinda slow and not ambitious, but you may get along well with a real spirited horse. They have personalities like you wouldn't believe, and they've got a spirit just like us. When you ride them, you can feel it between your legs and see it by the way they travel.

I had an old bay horse; I called him Sam. He got so used to working the gate at weaning time, he knew the difference between a cow and a calf and he didn't need you there. A horse like that you just kinda watch. Their spirit is so uplifting for me. I can be gloomy around the house and go out and ride, and it picks me right up, just like I slept all night. A lot of guys use horses as a tool, but they ain't a tool to me. They're a friend, and they got feelings, and they can hurt.

When you get caught in a storm, most times, a horse will take

Cows at watering hole

Rancher Roger Beierbach, Cypress Hills, Saskatchewan

you home. But if you ride into the wind, he ain't gonna want to go that way and will kinda circle around. You're still a lot better off to listen to him than to yourself. He's like a compass, and he's gotta go to that magnetic force. He will pack you through them storms and show you where you should or shouldn't cross the creek. And there's that sense of somebody there with you, somebody to visit with. You're never alone.

They are a person, really.

Roger Beierbach, rancher, Cypress Hills, Saskatchewan

Grandfather Turtle

We don't wear our braids just to look like Indians or to be cute. When I braid the left side of my hair where my spirit is strong, I hold three strands and ask that my mind, body and spirit work together in a good way, only for today. When I braid the other side of my hair, I take three strands again and ask that I'll have kindness, love and sharing with all people that I meet, only for today.

When I part my hair and make that path down the middle to the back of my head, I have to make that path straight because that's how straight I'll walk today. If my path is crooked as I'm going through my day, it might stay crooked. And I always make my hair as straight as I can so I'll walk, only for today, in a good way with all the people. When all is done and my braids hang nice and straight over each shoulder, they show the equality of man and woman, because they always hang nice and straight with each other.

If I pull only one of your hairs, I can break it, but I can't break the whole braid. That's how together we are to be with one another, and that's how we look at our braids. My son wore braids here in Dauphin, but it's unusual for a grade-four student to come to school with braids right down to his waist. And he got a lot of teasing, much of it from our native children. His name is Little Turtle, and his Grandfather Turtle, the spirit who watches over him, carries these braids on his back as well.

So I took my son to an elder, who said: "His spirit watches over him, but when a turtle is angry, he snaps. That's his defence. And Grandfather Turtle is very angry now because the people don't take the time to understand why this little boy is wearing braids, and they don't have any respect for him." Then the elder told me I should cut my son's braids for now because he's not strong enough to carry the weight of the meaning behind them.

So I took my son to a barber and got his hair cut off. I cried. The sadness was heavy inside me because he understood why he

Mary Bone, Strathclair, Manitoba

wore those braids but his peers and the community couldn't. He was very angry with people and was acting up in school. But maybe my expectations weighed too heavy on him. Now, he has short hair, and he's becoming more like himself again, making offerings to his Grandfather Turtle by putting tobacco on the fast water, asking for spiritual strength and thanking his grandfather for watching over him.

Linda Boudreau, youth referral worker, Dauphin, Manitoba

Playing deaf

One of our traditional Indian customs was grandparents helping with grandchildren. They always kept one, either a boy or a girl, and these grandchildren looked after their ageing grandparents. There's no way we would ever put our grandmother in an old people's home, even if we had to hire somebody to come and help us. She doesn't speak English, and she'd be so lonely, she wouldn't eat and would die from loneliness. It took a long time to make her understand that sometimes when she gets a chest condition or an upset tummy, we need to put her into the hospital until it's corrected.

Now, when she goes, she knows it's just a little visit, so she doesn't worry about it. Our nurses are very good. They have learned some basic words in our language so they can communicate with her. Every time she's there, they learn a new word, so the list is getting longer and longer. She laughs at them when they say these words. She says: "I play deaf. When the nurses are trying to talk my language, I fool them. I play deaf so they have to repeat it, then I chuckle away to myself because they can't say it right."

Julie Cochrane, retired farm worker, Strathclair, Manitoba

Prairie dog near Val Marie, Saskatchewan

Damming it all

There is talk of building a dam on the South Saskatchewan River just before the Red Deer River joins it. The dam will be devastating, but I'll be one of the few people who think that, because it's quite a badland area: rock, cliffs and not many trees along that stretch. Fabulous to look at but no economic value in it. Once you get a dam in, it would allow this whole country to be irrigated, and we're gonna lose all this prairie. You can't farm it now? It will be farmable with water.

Everything will change. In Alberta, they talk about irrigation creating habitat, about trees growing along the ditches. That's not the same, just a makeup for the things lost. But once the ditches overgrow, the water doesn't flow, so they rip the trees out, and it takes another 30 years for anything to grow back again.

Then it's not the prairie anymore; it's something else. What scares me about making parks, such as the Grasslands National Park, is that one day, we'll have these little patches here and there like they have in Europe, where hordes of people go to look at them. Don't worry, we've got this park here now; we've preserved something.

We just don't have the rest.

Dean Francis, artist, Mantario, Saskatchewan

Deer and geese on the South Saskatchewan River at sunset

Cattle grazing near Empress, Alberta

Young man excited

Soon after my father started his dairy farm, the diphtheria epidemic struck two winters in a row, and a lot of babies died. My father couldn't refuse anybody milk for their kids, but he wouldn't get paid, and life was difficult.

He came to Canada in 1908, but because he was a Frenchman, he was called back to do his duty in World War I. Rather than lose his French citizenship, he went to war, managed to survive, met my mother and brought her back in 1919. She came from a city in France and had a terribly hard time on the prairies, but my dad was a young man excited. It was all wild land with lots of Indians, and he liked that. For $10, he got a quarter-section on Meadow Lake, and as a veteran, he got another. That was a great thing, a lot of land, but my mother didn't like it. A terrible life. Wood stoves and no floor, just clay ground. No clothes. No city to go to. No people to see; that's what she missed. She adapted after a while but wanted to go back to France all her life.

It was hard for my parents to bring up seven children. Farming in the 1930s was a disaster. The rains didn't come. Heat and heat and heat. The crops were so poor, there were almost none. You had to get rangeland far away and use the kids to watch the cattle. The wells dried up, and in the morning, we had to bring our cattle to Backwater Creek, which was still flowing, then walk four miles to school.

Our dairy was just north of town, so people would come to us looking for work. We used to look through the window on a cold, blustery day and see one or two men walking in their thin old suit coats, knocking on the door and asking, ''Can you give us a job, any job?'' My mother would ask them in and feed them from a big pot of beans simmering on a huge wood stove, and if my dad was there, he would tell them, ''I'm sorry, I've got no money,'' and they'd have to walk back. But it's no use for me to tell that to my kids. They don't really believe we never saw apples.

In the Hungry Thirties, many people from the south had to leave their farms, but there was still free land in the bush around Meadow Lake, so they'd come north, and we were swamped by them. They'd go by with one or two cows tied behind the wagon with a tent on it.

When I was 18, I left to go to World War II. During the war, my dad got sick and sold his dairy for next to nothing. Because he was well educated, he got a job with the French embassy in Ottawa. My parents decided that as soon as the sons came back from the war, we'd all go back to France, then we'd be safe. All Euro-

peans were like that: they came here, found a harsh life and not much money, made the best of it, but one day, they wanted to sell and go back. The heck with Canada, it was just too terrible.

But when we came back from Europe, we told my parents we'd never go and live in France. France was a disaster, just horrible. People were starving. Everything was bombed. We weren't going back. Never. We were Canadians.

Herbert Bouillet, personnel manager, Gimli, Manitoba

I was raised in a family of women. My father died when I was 2, and my mother was devastated by his death. She had 43 cents left, but 10 days later, she went back to university to get her degree. She had to walk the length of Clarence Avenue at 6 o'clock every morning, and the janitor would let her in to get warm and to study till her first class started. She didn't cry that first year. She didn't cry until her graduation day in May.

On Saturday mornings, my mother gave art classes for professors' kids, and every winter, she had no money to buy me new shoes, but she always found money for books. Upstairs in the hallway, there was a linen closet that had no sheets and towels in it but two shelves of storybooks, and I wore a path from my bed to that closet. She was my first literary mentor.

On my first day of school, my mother gave me a yellow pencil and a five-cent scribbler. I still remember the woody smell of the paper, the feel of the pencil turning in my fingers and this terrible need to learn how to make letters so I could put words on paper. I wasn't so precocious that I ever thought of writing down the stories I was inventing. I sat closest to the window in school, always daydreaming. Teachers tried to knock it out of me but didn't succeed; if they had, I wouldn't be writing today.

My grandmother lived with us, and eventually, my Aunt Signe came too. She went back to university at age 50; being a dutiful farm wife, she didn't attend in the summertime because she had to cook for the threshers. She worked at the farmers' union so her husband didn't have to pay her way. My aunt also worked for the women's vote and was instrumental in bringing in the first provincial library. I identify with her strongly; she was like an Earth Mother to me, a vibrant, redheaded woman who would take me swimming in a mudhole under the bridge on the Turtle River.

I looked at men from a great distance, trying to figure them out. The men on the farm talked about me but never to me, as if I weren't there, and they were always in the field or else sleeping. Courtship and marriage brought wonderful surprises, but I had a lot of romantic nonsense to do away with and some harsh realities to deal with. My mother had idolized my father. He was absolutely perfect in every story she told me, but when I did something she didn't like, she would say, "Oh, you're just like your father." That was good; it made him human. From the time I was 13, I learned to love men for their flaws; my heroes always fell off their pedestals, always had clay feet.

Every woman in my family was able to muster residual strength in times of war, depression or personal tragedy and to go on, no matter what. The three I lived with and my paternal grandmother were very strong influences in my life. The Swedish mamas were nurturing like their bread—braided, with almond icing in the cracks—but my paternal grandmother was different. She was a Brit, a judge's daughter educated at the Sorbonne, who came from India to Edam, Saskatchewan, in 1900 with her husband, who didn't know how to grow anything but orange pekoe tea. She survived the Depression, but her husband had died, and she lived by bartering her music. She told the druggist, "I will teach your child piano or dance, violin, guitar or accordion if, when I need medicines, you'll give them to me free."

My grandmother went to the Duck Lake farmers and said the same thing. The son of the owner of the movie theatre had a speech impediment, so she offered to give him speech lessons in exchange for free admission to the movies. She took me many times, walking in like a lady and just nodding. On Sunday mornings, she got a free taxi ride to church because she also taught the taxi driver's kid.

She was a wonderful woman whom I didn't appreciate early enough in my life because she was an embarrassment to me. She was 4 foot 10 in her highest heels; in the summer, she wore a muskrat coat down to her ankles and an enormous black straw hat. To cheer herself up when she was blue, she would buy a bunch of silk violets and pin them on top of her hat. When the top brim got full, she began pinning them underneath. As you watched her coming down the street, all you could see was this brown fur with a mass of flowers on the top.

Every Christmas, she came to Saskatoon to be with us, and when we would go to the train station to meet her, we would see a frantic redcap coming up the steps clutching her little portmanteau, tied by one of her red belts, with clothing falling out of it.

Victorian memorabilia

She followed behind with the violin she had brought from France at the turn of the century tucked under her arm. When we got home, she would phone the Prime Minister, John Diefenbaker, who was always in Saskatoon at Christmas visiting his brother Elmer. She had campaigned for Diefy, as she called him, from his earliest days as a politician in Prince Albert and always had big posters of him in her window. She insisted I play the violin to him over the phone, and I would hide in the book closet to get away from this humiliating task; but she would stand at the foot of the stairs and holler and then drag me down. When I was in my thirties, I met Diefenbaker at a banquet, but I didn't tell him who my mother or grandmother was; I was still too embarrassed.

She aged beautifully. She seemed old as long as I can remember, but when Diefenbaker would visit her in Prince Albert, she would flirt with him. She would say, "Would you go into my chambers?" And he'd say, "Yes." And she would say, "Oh, you are naughty," and she'd hoist her skirts up and do the cancan from her youth in Paris, saying, "Those aren't bad legs for an old lady, are they?" According to her, he would throw back his head and roar with laughter.

She was such an eccentric and so demanding that it would have been impossible for my mother to have lived with her. She would bring her favourite violin pupil with her without asking if it was all right and would not allow her to help with the dishes because of her violin fingers. That upset the Swedish side of the family a lot. She would sit at the table, always holding court, and at the other end would be my shy little Swedish grandmother, who wouldn't say very much. My father's mother would say, "The other day, a lady came to my house; I'm not sure if she was Lutheran or CCF, but I didn't like her," knowing that my Swedish grandmother was both. When my parents married, they had to elope because she didn't approve. A Victorian snob is really what she was, yet very courageous, so it all made for the richest material possible in some of my novels. But, of course, I invent like mad and tell all sorts of lies, which often gets me into domestic trouble.

Byrna Barclay, writer, Regina, Saskatchewan

My old buck

I love deer probably more than anybody on Earth, and I hunt them too. I have grown through hunting and discovered that deer are smart, especially the big old bucks. They're strangely mysterious and cunning, and you learn to respect their ways and that mystery about them. You see the young ones all the time, but they don't get you excited like these old characters. When you finally see one, the feeling is tremendous: here's this magnificent animal, this son of a gun.

It's hard to shoot a deer, but the old bucks have only one or two years left in them. They're already starting to suffer, because their teeth wear out and they can't eat off the branches during the winter. But it isn't easy or fun to shoot them, and after you've done that, you feel really sad, especially with a deer you've known for some time. He's outwitted all the other hunters and somehow managed to survive.

I feel I know him, his qualities and his patterns. Sometimes I watch him coming out of the sagebrush, working on a ridge and looking ahead, being very careful as they always are, and all of a sudden, I'm not really sure what he's looking at. He could see more deer ahead or maybe a coyote. He gets me to think about what's going on, but it's just him and his world.

It's something they call "buck fever." Since you were a kid, you've spent some of your life with that big buck. And now, you squeeze the trigger, and it's over. You'll never forget him because you've known him all this time and then put an end to him. But if you don't get him, that old son of a gun is gonna have a terrible death, because he's got so weak, the coyotes will bring him down. Do you kill him after all this time and with all the respect you have for him, or do you let him starve to death, torn down by the coyotes chewing his hocks till he collapses? Finally, it will come down to you and him, way out there.

Dean Francis, artist, Mantario, Saskatchewan

Gift

My husband kept a three-quarter section of native prairie pasture, and in deer-hunting season, he wouldn't let anybody hunt on us. He was called quite a few names, none really complimentary, but he always thought that wildlife should have a place to live. Then on Father's Day, our daughter Nancy gave him a gift: an honorary deed for one acre of the Monteverde rainforest in Costa Rica. For $25, you can "buy" one acre down there and have it protected, because they are destroying it all. He sure was pleased, because some of our songbirds may go down there and have a place to winter without anybody bothering them.

Marjorie Robinson, retired farmer, Saskatoon, Saskatchewan

Mule deer at dusk, Milk River Valley, Alberta

Old chuckwagon in winter, Cypress Hills, Saskatchewan

Good life

We've been married 52 years. Graham brought me here in 1936, right in the worst of it. I was nice and slim then and wore a nice little white hat set on the side of my head and white slippers cut out fancy and white gloves and a white purse. I was happy, and Graham had the nicest red hair, just a mat with curls. Oh, we had a nice wedding in Maple Creek, very quiet, just about seven of us. Later, we went down to the restaurant and had a little supper and then came up in an old open Chevy car, just about running into a black cow. By the time we got over to Merry Flat school, neighbours were all set with a wedding dance for us, so we danced.

Then we came to our little log house down at Battle Creek. Some of the young folks had gone up on the roof earlier and plugged up the chimney, so when we tried to start a fire, it just about smoked us out. That first winter, the weather was so cold that some of the cows around the place just seemed to die standing up. Magpies froze to death too.

But we had a good life. Graham got me a nice, gentle saddle horse, and we used to ride together, here and there and everywhere. I don't think people worried about the little things half as much as they do today, and there was no money to think about. We didn't have all this TV, but you seldom went more than two days without a visitor, so there was nothing lonesome about it. I think this TV is the worst thing they ever did invent as far as the human race is concerned: it certainly broke up people visiting one another.

Modern people would be quite shocked to come to our little old house and find two or three persons sleeping on the floor in the kitchen and maybe a couple more in the barn, but we didn't think anything of it, just more people for breakfast. In the winter, we spent a lot of time skating and sleigh riding, and we'd think nothing of taking the sleigh four or five miles to find a good hill to ride on. We all danced and partied too. Those early people, they weren't what you'd think today, just straight work. They weren't built that way.

Laura Parsonage, retired rancher, Maple Creek, Saskatchewan

Laura and Graham Parsonage

The day of my 14th birthday was the end of my academic education. You had to be 14 before you could quit school, and I wanted to quit: I had a very sadistic principal who used to enjoy beating kids with a strap. I worked as a trucker for a hardware company, and when I was 15, I hired myself on as a fireman at the railroad to shovel coal on the steam engines. You had to be 21 by law, but it was 1918, the war was on, and anybody who was physically fit was already conscripted. I was a pretty fair-sized kid, so they told me to say I was 21, which I did.

The locomotives of those days devoured a lot of coal. You had to open the door, swing in about eight shovels, quickly shut the door, sit down for maybe 20 seconds and then shovel some more; sometimes you couldn't sit down at all. The longest shift I remember was 41 hours to cover 167 miles. It was a single track, and we had to meet another fellow coming the opposite way, but he had troubles, and we had to wait. It was winter, 40 below, the engine was leaking water, and by the time we tried to start our train, we couldn't. The axles got so congealed, the brakes stuck to them; so we had to take 10 cars for a half-mile run, warm them up, come back and get another 10 and then try to pick up the whole train. By that time, we were out of water, so we had to cut the engine away from the train and run for the water tank 15 miles away, then come back through a blizzard and find our train. It was a precarious job because if you didn't get water into the boiler soon enough, your engine could blow up and kill the crew, which often happened.

We had many ways of describing poor engines, but they weren't fit to put in a book. Conditions were grim. Because of the terrific heat of the firebox, you'd sweat and open the window just to get a blast of cold air. Some trains had no electricity, so the engineer had no light to read the orders by, and the fireman would hold the door open and make sure the orders weren't snatched out of his hand by the draft. We carried lumber, coal, sulphur and all the stuff from various mines. In the fall, the railways would put on as many crews as they could to move the bulk of wheat to the Lakehead before the freeze-up. During the 1930s, the trains were loaded with men looking for work. After they jumped aboard just outside of Moose Jaw, where they had tents, their extra weight would almost stop the train from going up the hill. Some tried to get on with loads on their backs, but it was such an awkward deal, they would often slip off and be killed.

The worst year on record was 1947, when the snow piled up as high as 30 feet. Trains froze up, and some had to be left until next summer. Once, we went out on a snowplough, taking with us 90 diggers with shovels; it was essential we get through because many people out there were out of coal and had no other means of heating their houses. The drifts were higher than the telegraph poles, and we got stuck too, so the diggers had to dig on different levels and scoop the snow up, but we'd only got halfway through this huge drift. We had three engines with us, and the superintendent asked me, "Jack, would you just hit this drift as hard as possible?" Unfortunately, speed on this track was limited to 20 miles an hour because its bed wasn't very strong, but we did go for it, going maybe 50 miles an hour with the roof of the drift caving in on us and the snow flying furiously into the caboose, so it looked like a spray room with a shower on. Finally, I yelled to the fireman, "Hang on, we're going to hit," and we did. I thought he might fall into the firebox with the impact, but we chugged down to our last breath and got through. The people from this town let go a big cheer, and we were happy too, just soaking wet.

Things happen on the railway. Once, we came into Regina with maybe 120 people on the train, doing 60 miles an hour. We had the green light, but suddenly, we saw a big black oil tanker that had been hit and knocked over on our track. There were three of us in the cab: the fireman, a CPR official on his first trip and myself. These two chaps hollered to me, "Plug'er! Plug'er!" But I didn't do it.

What "plug'er" means is shutting the power off, applying the brakes and stopping quick, but I knew I couldn't stop short of that tanker. Also, we had the old-type clasp brakes, steel rubbing on steel, which would make plenty of friction, and the flying sparks could ignite all that gasoline. We were going to be blown up, incinerated—not only my passengers but plenty of people in Re-

Canadian Pacific freight train near Brandon, Manitoba

gina. So I yanked the throttle out two more nicks, hit that tanker full speed and knocked it over. We went the other way, and I thought we were going to overturn, but we didn't. I ran by the station deliberately, because I didn't know what was happening behind me, and all I could think of was an inferno; but there was nobody injured, although many side windows were broken. We later learned the tanker was full of high-octane gasoline and was knocked over onto our track by a fellow coming from Saskatchewan. We were just oh so lucky to be alive.

Jack Pye, retired railroad engineer, Moose Jaw, Saskatchewan

We don't find it difficult, honest

The women in the colony work harder, because the men have everything push-button. They sit on a tractor all day in their air-conditioned cab, just steering. I don't say they're lazy, but we, the women, do everything with our hands and backs. Birth control is against our religion, so we have many children. We have to make all the clothes we wear. We stoop and cook and bake. We hoe the garden. We pick cucumbers. We wash the floor. We wash the clothes. The men don't care; they just come home and go to sleep in a clean bed, and what man would pick peas or cucumbers? The women work steady, and they work harder.

We never go to the colony's meetings. The men don't want us there because apostle Paul said in the Testament that only men should make decisions. It is our religion, and it has kept us alive for 400 years. If we want to say something, we can talk to our husbands at home. Men say: "We want to buy land. We want to buy a tractor. We want to build a pig barn." But that's not our business. Let them build a pig barn. I don't care, and I don't even ask.

The women make their own laws and regulations among themselves. Every week, they organize parties to make the noodles, to clean, to garden. Today, we're slaughtering chickens, and we know whose turn it is to cut the meat and who is to sweep the floor and fill those stainless-steel troughs with water so we can put the chickens in. Everything is so organized, you can't imagine. But we have our arguments, just like you have. We struggle; don't you think it's heaven. When there is an argument, we talk about it and take the majority's position.

We also have the power at home. Sometimes children have to be spanked, and the wife gets after her husband: "Why don't you

Barbara and Hilda Gross

26

Slaughtering chickens, Pincher Creek Hutterian Brethren Colony, Alberta

look after your children?'' because it's his part. I don't believe you can raise children without spanking. After my husband passed away, the strap was always on the table. I had to be a father and a mother to 13 children, and that was hard.

But it's a lovely way of life, and we are used to it. So quiet, no guards, no police, and people respect us. We don't find it difficult—honest. I'd have told you if it was.

Barbara Gross, Pincher Creek Hutterian Brethren Colony, Alberta

Abandoned farmhouse, Coteau Hills, Saskatchewan

Scavengers

There was no snow at all in the winter of 1948 until about April 10. Then the weather started to close in on us, and about five days later, a blizzard moved in. It was the worst one I've ever seen. It piled up drifts as high as 20 feet, covering all the telephone and power lines and everything else. Crews of farmers went out hand-shovelling the main road and the railroad tracks so the train could go through, and a lot of people could get food and mail only by plane.

We couldn't do anything. People on the farms, they just didn't move. There was an old man that lived south of my folks, an old bachelor, and a fellow in town who had an airplane flew the groceries out to him. The old man was to walk up to my dad's for the odd bit of milk, but he didn't, and when they found him quite a few days later, he was sitting in his chair, frozen.

There was a rumour that he had buried a considerable amount of money on his property, and for years afterward, people would go down there and dig around. It didn't seem to bother them that it wasn't their property they were walking in on.

One time, we met a young woman from town. She was telling us that on weekends, she and her husband and another couple would go out, find these old abandoned farmhouses, and while one of them stood guard, the others would go in to see what they could take. She said, "That's how we decorated our basement," and she didn't have any qualms about it. I just couldn't believe it.

Joanne Moulton, farmer, Hussar, Alberta

Farm for sale near Rockyford, Alberta

Cow bones, the Great Sand Hills, Saskatchewan

Palliser's Triangle

The history of the prairies is a very strange business. It started with John Palliser, leader of the British expedition in the 19th century, who declared that the southern prairie was uninhabitable and could not be developed for agriculture: it was too dry. Then at the turn of the century, the migration from central and eastern Europe brought thousands upon thousands of people who began to earn a living from the prairie soil, and Palliser was proved dead wrong. But in the 1930s, when the soil blew away, Palliser was proved right again. Then the farmers began to take careful measures to properly exploit the prairie and restore the content of the soil. When the generation who remembered the 1930s died, their children took over, and now they have become careless again.

Was Palliser right or wrong? One generation says, ''We've completely discredited him,'' and the next one says, ''Palliser has completely discredited them.'' But if you look at the history of northern Africa at the time of the Romans, you learn it was a breadbasket too, and then it became a desert. So was Mesopotamia, another great production area that is now just a desert. I suppose there must be instances of desert reclaimed.

The other day, I read a book about that part of the world, and I saw some pictures of Palmira, once a big trading city the size of Edmonton on the upper Euphrates or near it. It had tremendous markets and more statues of caravan leaders than of poets or generals, because they were the commercial people, but what's left today is a residue of streets, fragments of public buildings, and no one lives there at all. My son said no, cities don't completely disappear, and I said yes, they do. There is no such thing as permanent, and if we think we're building for eternity, we are wrong. We already know what the outcome of progress is going to be: zilch. And if life has any meaning at all, it has to be established on the basis of something else besides limitless human potential that we won't live to see. The whole direction of modern thought is that anything new must be better than anything old, and that's progress. But is it progress or disintegration?

Ted Byfield, publisher, Edmonton, Alberta

Evening in Dinosaur Provincial Park, Alberta

The coming of winter

I have a lot of birdhouses out, and four years ago, I made a dugout. I wanted some water so more birds would stay around. Sometimes on a Sunday afternoon, I just sit myself down there in the willows and watch. There is a regular bird relay for a drink. I see the crows, the robins, the blackbirds, the goldfinches, the

I see the birds

My father was a grain elevator agent, but he didn't enjoy his last years there. He had to deal with young farmers who were pretty hard-nosed businessmen and didn't care if they were faithful to him or if they left him to look for a better price.

Many farmers feel hard-pressed; they've got huge loans for big machinery and high-priced land, so they look for the best deal they can. They break up all the land and bulldoze the bush. I hate a bare field because it's very boring, and if I was bored, I wouldn't be at this job. So I save as much bush as I can, and I like to look at it as I work around it with a tractor. I see the birds and the deer, and there's always a fox, but all winter long, he makes darn sure you don't see that red against the snow.

I like spring best. You can smell that moist land, and the first joy of spring is to hear the horned larks come back with their tinkling welcome before the snow is even gone. And soon after the meadowlark returns, we get very busy. That's the worst part of farming: when spring is in full bloom, you're sitting on a big tractor with the cab separating you from nature. I rode on an open tractor for 25 years and heard every bird as I passed by, but these new machines are just too noisy. We're too soon old and too late smart.

Lawrence Beckie, farmer, Kenaston, Saskatchewan

White swans during fall migration near Smiley, Saskatchewan

mourning doves and even the horned larks from the fields. The vesper sparrow and the meadowlark are our longest song-stresses; they quit singing about the middle of July, and then the quiet sets in, and the heat is on. But I already see the blackbirds flocking, and I know many birds will soon be gone. The winter is coming. I feel just like a drunk or a drug addict might feel—a sense of withdrawal. It's a depressing time until you get set in for winter or just plain accept it.

Lawrence Beckie, farmer, Kenaston, Saskatchewan

Roping practice, Pincher Creek Hutterian Brethren Colony, Alberta

Tougher every year

This calf died a couple of hours ago. I thought it had laryngitis, so I brought it to the vet to check it out, but now we found out it had eaten a plastic bag. Calves are like that; they like to pick up anything: it could be twine, it could be twigs. But I thought it was a disease, and I've got 11 more calves left, so I worried.

We haven't had any rain for months, pastures are drying out, crops are poor, and if we don't get rain by the first of July, we're going to have nothing. It's not easy, but what else can we do? I like to farm. It's been in me for a lifetime, cattle and everything, and I'm 42. It would be hard to leave now.

I'm only on a quarter section, a small farm. Ducks, geese, chickens, a little bit of grain, a bit of alfalfa, and the rest is pasture. Mostly animals. Oh, yes, and wildlife too. I like that, wildlife. I like big animals and ducks, wild geese.

I used to hunt, but I quit because everything is running out. I used to trap muskrats, mink, some foxes, an odd coyote, maybe one or two lynx, weasels and squirrels, but I don't anymore. I just like to see wild animals around, but the fertilizers and the sprays hurt them. If they hurt people, how are they not going to hurt the animals? Weasels are pretty near extinct out here.

Farming is not easy, and it's getting tougher every year. Our machinery is all small and old. And to buy anything new, now? There's no way. We can't afford it. Even selling the house, it wouldn't help. Everything is difficult. The drought. Your repairs. Even used machinery is getting fairly high. It's very hard. There'll be no crops and hardly any hay this year. There will be no more trucking. We just have to make sure we can bring in what we've got left for the winter.

Lawrence Zurbyk, farmer, Elphinstone, Manitoba

Lawrence Zurbyk and pig

This wall took 27 years out of my life. It's about a half-mile long, and it took maybe two million stones to build. It's over six feet tall and mostly seven feet wide in the bottom. I didn't do it to become famous, but you have to be me to understand the things I do. The idea started a long time ago. Us kids, we all had to work, because at that time, we weren't here just for the fun of it. I had to herd cattle out on the prairie, so I would go on top of a knoll and take something along to pry the rocks out. Then I would pile them up in a V shape, and when the wind blew, I could lean on this side. When it got hot, I could lean on the other side. That might have been it.

I also wanted to leave something so my children and, later, their kids could come back after I'm gone and talk about me. It would be like a homecoming for them. That way, I'd still be alive. That's about it, because the wall doesn't hold anything in and it doesn't hold anything out. And there is no profit in it.

To build it, you couldn't have a bad back, you couldn't have a bad heart, and you had to be in a privileged position to afford it. For some people, everything they touch turns to gold, don't it? Maybe I was one of them. Not that I knew more than other people did, but I seem to have done the right things in my life. Some people never do; whatever they try, something goes wrong. But the harder I worked, the luckier I got.

The stones came from about a five-mile radius. They all had to be hauled in, and it cost me money, machines—front-end loader and backhoe. Where did I get the money from? I've got oil wells all over this place. Pretty easy, eh? But I didn't put the oil here; it just happened to be under where I was. My people came from the States, but it was pretty rough in Saskatchewan in those days, and my family went back to Minnesota to a nicer climate and nicer roads. I stayed. Now, was I lucky or just a little bit more determined? You can call it luck if you want to.

How did I start? There's a slough down here, and the land alongside is nice and sandy. I thought it was a good place to grow corn, so we picked up stones and dumped them on the top of the hill. I thought it looked pretty homely, so I started piling them up. People were curious, so after I got pretty far, I told my boy: "It looks like we're getting enough attraction here; maybe we better make it as good as we can. If people are coming from a long ways away, we want them to see something they can talk about." I built it sharp on top, but when school buses started to come, the kids wanted to walk on it, so I had to make it wider. It took me six months to change, and now, you can walk on it from one end to the other. I hope nothing happens; it hasn't so far.

My neighbours called me crazy, and I had to quit paying attention. You don't do stuff like this without a little comeback—no way. My wife was also put out by my spending so much time here; we could be going someplace, doing other things. But I said: "This is my thing. I've got to do it." She couldn't have stopped me no matter what she'd done.

I quit last year, and now it seems like a dream. I could've kept on working till I died, but I didn't want to. The guy who did Mount Rushmore never finished; he died. There was also a fellow south of Moose Jaw who thought we were going to have another flood. He built this good-sized ship out on the prairie, 12 miles from the river. He's dead too, but we had something in common, even if he was crazier than me.

I never paid awful much attention until it was all done, but when I looked at the whole thing, I said, "How stupid could I get, to work for 27 years on that?" But the public comes here, and I get in the papers, and that's enough for me. Most people who came into this country 50 years ago are completely forgot about. They came, went, left nothing, and their names are gone. Some say they pioneered this country and broke the ground, but they didn't come here because they wanted to make this country better. Their bottom line was money, and they didn't worry about what they destroyed. Why should I be different? My bottom line isn't money, just this wall, and for the last two years, I've had about 4,000 people come here just to see it. I suppose I could've robbed a bank or killed a couple of people and still have my name in the paper, but I think I've accomplished something important, even if it's just with stones. My name will never die.

Albert Johnson, farmer, Smiley, Saskatchewan

Albert Johnson and his stone wall, near Smiley, Saskatchewan

"Colourful Ribbon Dance" at Folklorama Festival, Winnipeg, Manitoba

We Canadians are a strange race

Canadians are always trying to find out who they are. Is our identity half French and half English or, perhaps, multicultural? We are quite lost. If you were to ask me what is the Canadian identity, I'd say it's 30 percent anti-British, 30 percent anti-American and 40 percent bugger-all. We're always in a political crisis over some new regulation concerning either language or the metric system, and in most beer bars, people end up talking about identity. It's a pain in the neck.

I don't know how we're going to use two languages without getting them mongrelized, but we're supposed to turn ourselves into a totally bilingual society. That doesn't go down very well with a lot of Westerners. To silence that kind of opposition, we've adopted the multiculturalism policy and have endless programmes for the Germans, the Ukrainians, the Filipinos and everybody else. Winnipeg is now the Folklorama City: we started this damn thing, and now, every year, we have a festival that goes on for two weeks. You hear all the songs and see the dances and eat different food, and what the hell, it's fun. But beyond that, there are serious problems. As soon as people want to do any kind of a folk dance, they immediately demand a state subsidy, claiming it will create another facet of Canadian identity. I say if you've got anything worth doing, just do it.

We Canadians are a strange race in many respects. We got everything for nothing and didn't have to raise a finger or do a damn thing. We didn't have to win our independence or win the West. The Brits did it all for us, and we can't even show gratitude because that is considered real dirty. Perhaps we envy the people from the United States, and it makes it embarrassing that they also speak English. If only the damn Americans had invented a new language when they got their independence, everybody up here would have been really happy.

They should have spoken Esperanto.

Eric Wells, news commentator, Winnipeg, Manitoba

Indian dancers at Folklorama, Winnipeg, Manitoba

herd, there must have been incredible waste, because how much meat can you eat? But when you learn how the culture of the Plains Indians worked, you realize there was no waste. A band would follow a herd and pick off one animal, usually older, or people would get together with other bands and do a buffalo jump. They would count how many buffalo there were so there would be one for every family unit, but they never took the meat from a few animals and left the rest to rot.

It was a surprise for me to learn that. I remember meeting an archaeological crew from the University of Calgary near the jump, and one of the women escorted our group to the base of the cliff. She pointed out it wasn't very high, only 30 feet or so,

Head-Smashed-In

Native culture in the prairies is a love and hate thing. You see native people struggling to survive in the cities, and there's a lot of tragedy and sadness. And yet in the prairies, unlike in other parts of Canada, you see native people every day. They're part of this society. I know where I can go in Toronto to see a native Indian, because there's a Native Friendship Centre, but you almost never see Indians in the streets: they are invisible. In the prairies, you get exposed to native culture very naturally.

White people tend to think about European history as the only history here, but when I went to Head-Smashed-In Buffalo Jump in southern Alberta, where the Indians used to stampede entire herds of buffalo off the cliffs, I suddenly saw the human history of the prairies very differently. You assume Head-Smashed-In Buffalo Jump got its name from the buffalo going over the cliffs and smashing their heads in. That's not true. It came from a brave who was waiting below the jump, became impatient and climbed the cliff just as the buffalo started to come over. I remember thinking, rather impishly, that this contradicts the romantic image of the Indians as totally ecological people: if they would kill a whole

Bison and full moon on Schmalzbauer Buffalo Range, Hoosier, Saskatchewan

and everyone agreed it seemed very low. ''That's because you're standing on 75 feet of buffalo bones,'' she said.

That spot had been used as a buffalo jump for 3,000 years. It was easy to look out on the plains from the base of the cliff and imagine these herds of buffalo with bands of Indians following them. And suddenly, I got a sense of how old the human history of this place was.

Jars Balan, poet, writer, teacher, Edmonton, Alberta

Bread

I was collecting material for a historical book about this area, and one woman told me how she and her husband were madly in love back in Norway. He came to the prairie to get a little bit of money together and got to be a manager of a large farm. When she arrived, he went to Saskatoon to meet her on the train and brought her back to the farm. It was just a dirty old shack, and she had come from a city in Norway where they had running water and electricity and even gas. She just sat and cried.

He brought a 155-pound sack of flour from town, and she had never seen a flour bag that big in her life. He said he was going

Making candles, Lower Fort Garry National Park

to work early in the morning and she was to bake bread while he was gone. If she needed help, there was a Norwegian lady down the road about three miles, and she could ride over on the horse and talk to her. You see, she couldn't speak a word of English.

She didn't admit to her husband that she didn't know how to bake bread, but after he left, she rode to see this neighbour, who told her to take a pail of flour and this and that. She never realized that this recipe was for 30 loaves of bread; so she went home, took all this flour, and by the time she put in enough water to make it wet, she had a big round oak table solid with bread dough. The woman forgot to tell her that you had to put the cake of yeast in water and soak it first, so she cut this hard yeast and just stuck it in. Of course, the bread wouldn't rise.

Finally, she tried to get the stove to burn. There hadn't been a fire in it for three or four years, so it was all smoke, but finally, she got it going and put four loaves in. Well, the bread wouldn't even turn brown, because it hadn't risen yet. She burst out crying, took the loaves and threw them to the pigs by a big slough full of water, but the loaves were so hard, the pigs wouldn't even look at them. Then she took this whole lot of dough and threw it down in the slough too. It was a hot July evening.

She jumped on the horse to borrow some bread for supper, but her husband didn't come home until late. He came home and saw all this bread rising in the slough and floating, white in the moonlight, along the shore. He thought the pigs had got out, so he went in and woke her up to help him put them in.

When they returned to the house, all he said was, "Damn it, woman, can't you do anything?" and went to bed. She told me she cried all night, and she had never been so lonesome or blue in her life. If she had only had the money to go home, she would have gone.

Elmer Sira, farmer, Hanley, Saskatchewan

Grain elevators, Vulcan, Alberta

Justifying

There are windfall years, and there are disastrous years, but every farmer justifies everything he does, while his neighbour says he's crazy and has a pack of his own reasons for doing exactly the opposite. They both sound valid. Everybody has pride in what he does, and if you tell him nose to nose, ''You've made a mistake,'' that's an insult. You've got to be awful careful how you give advice and how not to leave yourself wide open by saying you guarantee anything, because you can't. And if something you suggested to another farmer turns out wrong, he's going to come back madder than hell.

Ian McPhadden, farmer, Milden, Saskatchewan

Today, the only signs of early habitation on the remaining virgin prairie are parallel ruts in the grass; sometimes they are barely visible. They are half the width of the Red River carts settlers used; when the carts bogged down, drivers moved them half their width to straddle the rut.

Many people set up dwellings based on memories of their homeland. They knew how to build them, and it was a comfort to have something of your own in a new land. These first structures were made with what was available: lumber, mud, manure and straw. Some people used prairie sod, but life inside these huts must have been incredible. They were cool in the summer and warm in the winter, yet when it rained hard, the water would saturate the roof and drip inside for days. Eventually, prairie architecture began to depend on the manufactured products and buildings ordered from the Eaton's and Simpsons' catalogues. People were trying to attract others to settle in their communities, and these new houses gave an immediate impression of prosperity.

In the more substantial public buildings, you can still see civic pride and a sense of optimism. The people were making a personal statement: they were here to stay. And although many of them were subsistence farmers, others, attracted by the business potential, were rather wealthy and built substantial residences, often beautifully ornate inside. Churches provided a meeting place for people of similar ideas and offered comfort in a harsh landscape because prairie people, although strongly individual, relied very much on one another. People built to meet their needs: often, they'd build one half of a school; if the community didn't grow, they never added the other half.

Every town had a predictable collection of buildings: there was always a railway station, a bank and a town hall, a restaurant and a hotel. Generally, the railway would come first, but people knew it was coming and would build the town in anticipation of its arrival. Sometimes they were fooled, and they had to pick up the town and move it. Some towns grew to service the needs of the railway, which required watering tanks every so many miles.

Others serviced the needs of the farmers, who had to bring their grain wagons to elevators and return home within one day.

When you drive through the prairie landscape, you can learn a lot as long as you understand the language of the buildings. The number of grain elevators tells you how prosperous the community is, and if the ball is up on the water tank, you know it's ready to service an incoming train. They are just symbols, but we may be the last generation to see them. The wagons have been replaced by grain trucks, a great many elevators are scheduled for demolition, and the entire face of architecture in the prairies will soon change.

One of my favourite buildings is a one-room schoolhouse in the middle of prairie grassland near Kenaston. In the centre of the structure is a tower. There is a door at the base of the tower, and above that ordinary door with a curved top, there is a big fan of boards very neatly lapped one over the other and brightly painted in all the colours of the rainbow. Such buildings are grand, because you know people didn't slap them together just to keep the rain out.

I can imagine the people who used to live around Sunrise School a long time ago. They set up their schools, their churches and virtually their own society. When their children went to school, it was with the hope that they would have a brighter future. And every time those kids came in, they'd walk under that sunrise of a better tomorrow. I feel the farmers who built this small school understood the meaning of architecture. We tend to think it has to be expressed in an expensive, elaborate way; they did it simply by fanning out coloured boards over a doorway.

In folk and vernacular architecture, I can identify tool marks that tell me more about the people who lived in and used these structures than classical, imported forms ever would. And I like things that respond well to the needs at hand, such as the shelterbelt windbreak. It works. It breaks the harshness of the prairie. It gives shade and psychological enclosure. It provides the sound of the rustling leaves.

Wayne Zelmer, restoration architect, Regina, Saskatchewan

Making it

A tractor costs more now than I paid for the farm. If things get worse, I'll just float along like everybody else or do more welding. But even this is tough; nobody has money to spend, and it takes an average farmer $30,000 to put the crop in. When I was getting this place, I said, ''I'm not losing this farm, whatever it takes,'' and that was my priority for 15 years. But today, I wonder if it really paid off. I've had two hernia operations, two back operations, and I wonder if I didn't put too much stress on my own system. My family, they suffered too, and my wife wasn't happy about the things that we missed together.

I think a person has to sacrifice a lot for something he really wants to do.

Norman Tuplin, farmer, Beechy, Saskatchewan

Mud

I couldn't believe how sticky this Red River clay was when he first took me home. He was driving as fast as he possibly could down this wet road, and I thought he was trying to kill me even before we got married. Where I came from, we had light, sandy soil and we drove as slowly as possible, but if you drive slowly here, you get stuck and there's no way you can get out of it. You have to take the wheels off to clean out the mud because your fenders fill up.

This mud becomes rock hard when it dries. It is so sticky that when you walk across the yard after a rain, you must keep moving, because once you quit, you are stuck. One year, we planted trees on the field. It was wet, and I stayed in one spot too long, and my boots would not move. I had to get out of them and plant the rest in my bare feet.

When I was expecting our first child, I thought: "What if it rains? How am I going to get to the hospital?" It was July, the men were haying, we had no phone, and I had absolute horrors. So my neighbour and I set up a code that if I went into labour, I would go outside and wave a white flag and she would telephone the doctor and get the men from the field.

Betty Schlichting, farmer, Sanford, Manitoba

Fields and farm buildings, the Wintering Hills, Alberta

Prairie farmland during harvesttime, Wood Mountain region, Saskatchewan

People's taxes

I came to Saskatchewan because I was interested in the political party which was in power at that time, the Co-operative Commonwealth Federation. Its successor is the New Democratic Party. I was a young, unmarried lawyer with no intention of staying: Regina in 1950 was the end of the world, particularly if one had grown up in a prosperous little town in Nova Scotia. But in 1960, I was elected to the provincial cabinet.

At first, I was appalled by the wooden sidewalks, gravel streets and little privies out in the back. One could go on a paved road only from Regina to Moose Jaw. When this country was settled, all the land was surveyed into one-square-mile, or 640-acre, blocks called sections, and between sections, there were strips of land called road allowances. If you wanted to go northwest to Saskatoon, you had to go north, west, north, west, north, west. In 1944, there wouldn't have been a hundred farms in Saskatchewan with electricity from a line.

After the war, the government had no resources to build the infrastructure. It solved the problem by raising taxes. I suppose people are never happy to pay taxes, but they were happy enough to see new roads, schools and hospitals. The so-called left-wing governments in this province have always been conservative financiers, and the government I led had 11 straight surplus years.

Our political philosophy came from a grass-roots movement. After the war, there was a good deal of idealism. People were talking about freedom from fear and about the needs of the less able and the disadvantaged. The model called for a high level of social services and accessible education. By and large, that's happened, and although it gets eroded when a right-wing government is in, it doesn't get wiped out. The prairie wheat growers sell on world markets and cannot dictate their prices, but they don't have to have railway freight rates dictated by railway companies in Toronto. They don't have to have power or insurance companies located in the far distance running their lives.

Saskatchewan is probably the most politicized piece of ground in North America. During a provincial election, voter turnout is rarely under 80 percent. I have always thought people came to political meetings because they'd been out on their tractors alone and simply wanted to see another human being, but the idea that people can get together and solve their own problems is just part of the Saskatchewan ethos, and it doesn't exist in many other places in the world.

Right-wing politicians like to portray taxes as a deprivation of your right to spend your money, but I always want to say: ''Fine, get up in the morning, but don't use anything that's provided by tax dollars. Don't touch the water from your tap. Be careful of the electricity, and don't use the sidewalk, because they're all paid for with people's taxes. Just go about your business, and don't take advantage of the taxes while you're knocking them.'' And I think that politician would have a very difficult day.

Allan Blakeney, former premier, Regina, Saskatchewan

Dale Friesen, Piapot, Saskatchewan

do something physical, but I also feel the whole spiritual part of my brain clicking right into magic.

The summer sky is the landscape here, the place where everybody gets touched. When you lie on your back in the grass, you get a sense of the world being big and round, but you don't have to fight the bigness of it. You belong here, just the way a star looks tiny but you know it belongs up there. You feel small but not insignificant, and you realize how, within the big whole world, there are all these little wholenesses, both animal and human. And you feel whole.

It just knocks your socks off. Wow.

Heather Redfern, designer, Edmonton, Alberta

Boy and his cat, Winnipeg, Manitoba

Summary

There are two wonderful things about prairie summer—the long days and the way things grow. I go out in the morning to thin my beets, and a week later, I have beets ready to eat. I never had a garden before I came here, and it gives me a real sense of having to hurry, because soon, it's going to be cold.

I'm a different person in the summer. The long day turns on all my creative knobs. The pictures I want to paint may not be about that sky or about that long day, but the light gets me excited. I want to paint and feel the earth in the garden. I need to

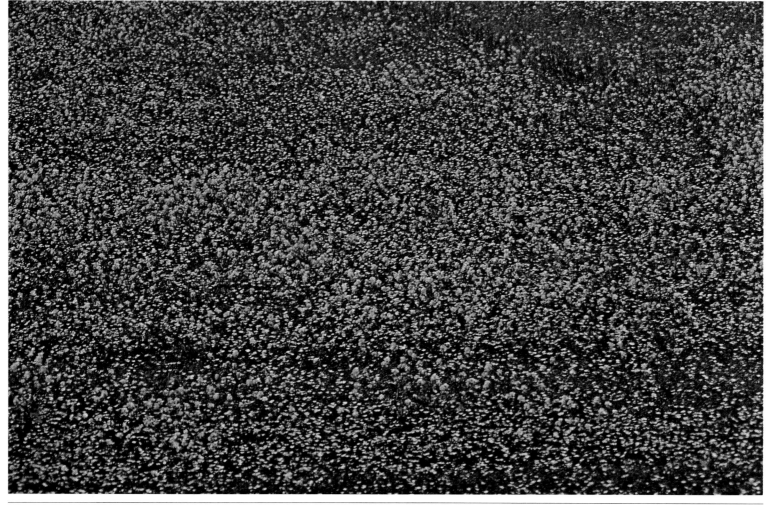

Flax field, southern Manitoba

Children at lunch, Pincher Creek Hutterian Brethren Colony, Alberta

We are like the bees

Many people have tried to live in a Hutterite community, but they say it's impossible: you have to be born in a colony; otherwise, you can't make it. A kindergarten is the ideal place to grow up. There, children play together, eat together, sleep together; they give their toys to each other and even share their candy. That's where community starts.

Our girls never say, ''Gosh, I'd like to be dressed like her,'' because we all dress alike, and when you know you can't have something, you haven't got the longing. If the boys aren't satisfied with the way we live, they go out in the world. They know it's hard. Here, they come from work, and the table is set; but when they leave the colony, they have to work hard to eat. I had a brother who joined the Marines. Once, he came home for a visit and said, "Many a time I wished for a piece of bread when I went to bed hungry."

I had eight boys and five girls, but even to this day, they do what I tell them and never talk back. The boys would sometimes sneak away, but the girls would always tell me where they were going and go to bed at 9 o'clock. Now, I have 44 grandchildren, and all my sons are still here, but I'm not proud or anything. We shouldn't be proud. One day, when we get up to 120 people, we'll have to split the colony, because those push-button machines don't take many people to operate them, and there won't be enough work for everybody. So we have to save money—not thousands, but millions; it takes an awful lot of money to build a new colony.

We take care of our old people until they die, but we also teach our children we all have to pitch in and don't want any lazy ones around. Just like the bees: if they find a lazy one, out, out, out of the hive. The colony is the same; we don't want no slow ones. They're looked upon real bad, and nobody likes them. I'm 73, and I still do what I can. I also tell my children, "The garden lady said you must go hoeing, so don't sit around and talk, go." Because if we are lazy, who will fill our freezer and the cooler? The winter is long.

When I was a girl and there was no school in the summer, my dad, who was a minister and my teacher, would take us three miles into a big field to pull the weeds. He watched us, and if somebody fell behind, he'd say, "Why aren't you like the rest, out in front?" Our parents teach the children, and that's why we need no education. Paul, the chicken man, has three boys, and

I say to him: "Remember, don't let them out of your sight. Go with them to gather eggs. They are your children; train them." Eddie, the pig man, takes his kids down to the barn to teach them. The cow man does the same, and all our girls help their mothers. We have education right here in the colony. I call it self-experience.

Barbara Gross, Pincher Creek Hutterian Brethren Colony, Alberta

The land makes me paint

The more time I spend out in the hills, the more this land means to me. Its beauty is in the strange and wonderful feeling I get from it. Not just the light and the colours and the shapes but that feeling as well. Other people say: ''You should go up north. Go east. Go west. Go to the mountains.'' I do go to those places, but they don't do it for me. I can go to the mountains and see tremendous beauty, but it's just not the same. It's not in my blood. But when I go out to the river hills and find a place that excites me, I forget about everything.

I usually go to the hills in the dark, when the deer move back to the trees. I set up a spotting scope and watch the wildlife until the morning movement is over, then pick up my stuff and walk through the woods or the hills. I usually take a camera. Not many

Autumn, Cypress Hills, Saskatchewan

Bare autumn trees, Wood Mountain, Saskatchewan

of those ideas turn out, because the camera probably kills a lot of that.

I paint because the land makes me paint. Painting doesn't make me look at the land; I think it's the other way around. I have not recorded the best moments on canvas or film because I haven't been able to do it. But it doesn't matter what I do with this land—whether I photograph it, paint it or just go out there—there's always more to it. It's a lifelong quest.

Dean Francis, artist, Mantario, Saskatchewan

My mom was Polish, and Dad was Ukrainian, but they met in Moose Jaw. My father worked for the Robin Hood Mills for years, until mechanization set in and he got laid off. After that, they went farming. You can farm even if you can't talk in English.

I first met Frank, my husband, at a christening at my aunt's. I was 16, but when he was introduced to me, he bowed and kissed my hand. I thought, ''Well, I'm just like a princess.'' That really did it. Two weeks later, I went back to my aunt's, and he came with another Polish fellow, a tailor's helper from Mossbank. They rapped on the door, and when I opened it . . . well, his eyes got so large, and he was just shocked. His friend said to me, ''He's been pining for you all week, but he didn't know how to meet you again.''

He started courting me but had no car and had to rent one to come up. It cost him $10 every Sunday. He worked in a large place where they were mining salt, and he was shoeing their horses and putting new tires on wagons. He didn't bring me flowers, but he bought me candy. In the wintertime, he wanted me to write him, but I said I couldn't walk to town to post my letters because I didn't have any overshoes; so he sent me a pair. He was very handsome; I guess that's why I fell for him, although he was 12 years older.

In 1931, he asked my parents if he could marry me, and they said no, they couldn't afford a wedding; but he said he would help out. He borrowed lumber from the lumberyard to build a big hall so the sun wouldn't beat on us, and I remember my mom killing an awful lot of turkeys and geese. People knew it was a Ukrainian-Polish wedding, so they all came, and my mom ran out of food. My husband had to go to Mossbank and buy up all the meat the butcher had to finish our wedding.

He always worked awfully hard. He shod horses and fixed wagons, charging a dollar a wheel, and if something had broken down and the farmers couldn't get it from the factory or from Toronto in a short time, they'd bring him the pieces, and he'd put them together somehow. There was hardly anything he couldn't do. We only had a two-room home, but that house was always full of people. We lived a good life. We weren't rich, but we had our own garden, our own pigs, our own honey. He took pigs in trade, chickens in trade. Even for our wedding, one poor old blacksmith gave us two ducks and a gander.

Until our son was born, he was forever whistling; when he'd get up in the morning, it was almost as if he were a nightingale. We were married 13 years before our son was born, but it seemed like when it finally happened, this happiness went out of him. No, it wasn't that. He just saw that his son should have a better life than he did. He loved him very much, and whenever the boy talked back, he'd say nothing to him. Afterward, he'd just say, ''Oh, my son, my son . . .'' But the whistling stopped.

About 14 years ago, my husband had a bad accident. He and our son Michel were working on a truck, and then Michel started it up. And all of a sudden, my husband stepped right in front of the truck, and my son ran over him, jamming his legs between the dual tires. ''Please,'' I yelled, ''somebody get a jack.'' The jack lifted the truck, but the wheels wouldn't go high enough. One man ran to get a tractor with a front-end loader, but in the meantime, his wife and I grabbed Frank and pulled him out.

His leg was broken open so you could see the bare bone, but in no time, the doctor wanted to discharge him from the hospital. I said, ''His leg isn't healed up,'' and the doctor explained that my husband wouldn't listen to the nurses and they didn't want to look after him. I said, ''Please, let him go home on a Sunday.'' He said, ''Why on a Sunday?'' And I said, ''Because if my son brings him home on Saturday, all his friends will come with liquor, and there'll be no end to it.''

I used to go into his shop a lot and saw that farmers knew how to make him work at all times. He liked his beer, there was no doubt about it. I used to ring a cowbell for him to come for dinner, but one time, he didn't come, so I went to see. All the farmers were drinking beer, and Frank was at the forge with his anvil, banging like crazy and the perspiration running off him. I said to the farmers: ''You gentlemen are killing my husband with your kindness. Would you mind going home for dinner so he can have a bite to eat? Your wives are waiting for you too.''

He worked hard, even after his first heart seizure. I was watch-

Russo-Greek Orthodox wedding

ing him, but he said, "I love my work; just leave me be." Then one evening, something just twisted him right around. I managed to help him to bed, and we took him into the emergency in the morning.

After the operation, he came home but seemed to be getting weaker from the blood thinners. He couldn't eat, and he was already 84. The priest came over and said, "Frank, you've had a good life." And Frank said, "It's all been too short."

When we knew he was going to die, I asked him if he would like his body to be shipped back home. But he said: "Poland? It didn't give me nothing. This is where I made my life. I want to be buried behind the chokecherry trees in Mossbank."

I think if I lived my life again, I'd probably do it better. For instance, he never let me drive our car, because he had an old-country idea that women are dumber. If I could live again, I would also have us talk things over and say: "Listen here, you can't always be at the top. Let's go 50-50." But at that time, I just let him have his way. If I were more aggressive, my husband would just pound on his anvil and forget what I said. What are you to do with a man like that?

The idea of turning his shop into a museum came from my nephew. It took years to happen, but today was a big day: all these people came, and I cut the ribbon to open it. All I said was that on behalf of my children and myself, I want to present the blacksmith shop of Frank Ambroz, our beloved husband, father and grandpa, to the Mossbank museum. I don't even know what in the world I said; I just wasn't going to break down. My husband was tough and wouldn't cry for any little thing. But later, I called my friend to relieve a bit of the tightness in my chest.

Before he died, he said, "I suppose you'll forget me and never even come to see my grave." And I told him: "I'll never forget you, and as long as I'm in Mossbank, I will visit your grave. I know you won't be there in person, but you may be in the wind, maybe someplace in the sky. Your spirit will be with me always." The museum is really for him. I know he is proud when he looks down and sees how many people still remember the work he did for them.

Mary Ambroz, homemaker, Mossbank, Saskatchewan

On a river in the middle of a prairie

The Red River is a very old river. It starts in Minnesota and winds its way up to Lake Winnipeg, the only river flowing north out of the continental United States. In the spring, the melting forces the ice on its way north, and the ice is three to four feet thick, moving along and roaring with a tremendous force: it can uproot big trees and smash everything in its path.

I grew up on the river farmland, way down at the water's edge. As a kid, I would stand along the river, watching it and picking up lumber and boats that used to float by. We walked to school along the riverbank every day and had to go across the river in a rowboat to catch the bus to go to town. It was dangerous when it got really stormy, and I had a lot of respect for the river. I used to watch all the freighters going out to the lake. There'd be boats bringing in fish to Winnipeg and a lot of pulp and lumber coming in from the islands up north. It always intrigued me, so in 1969, my brother and I decided to get into the tour business. We bought the *Paddlewheel Queen*, and I've run her ever since.

In the springtime, we haul children, senior citizens and handicapped people; later, we haul tourists from all over the world. The *Paddlewheel Queen* is one of the major tourist attractions in Winnipeg, because river excursions on the prairies are pretty unique: we're in the heart of the North American continent. The dinner cruise is the nicest. You get the daylight as you leave, you get the dusk at the sunset, and you get the dark as you come back.

Last year, a promoter brought 25 American hunters from the States. He wanted to take them up to the mouth of the river and hunt ducks like from a floating hotel. He hired hunting guides who knew the marsh, which is a huge place. I brought my chef, and we had a roast suckling pig and buffalo steak; everything was first class, gourmet.

After the Americans loaded their hunting boats, dogs, guns and sleeping bags, the *Queen*'s main deck was almost full. It got

Boys fishing on prairie wetlands near Brandon, Manitoba

really cold and windy, and I wanted to get to the lake before night, but we lost a blade on one propeller, and by the time we got halfway down, it was dark. It was blowing and raining, the waves were getting big, and it was miserable. That night, I woke up my mate, and I said, ''We better check the boat; the wind just dropped,'' and sure enough, she was stuck on a mud bar. We pumped our bilges out and finally worked her loose.

The boat was a total disaster. There was mud and dirt everywhere, and the guys just butted their cigarettes and cigars all over the place. We got 21 ducks for 25 hunters, and that was the worst weather we had that year.

Steve Hawczuk, Winnipeg, Manitoba

Water park in West Edmonton Mall, Alberta

Have you been to West Edmonton Mall?

At West Edmonton Mall, we're offered a wonderful artificial world, a hall of distorted mirrors. The sounds and the sights that assault us are all part of a very controlled environment, like a television studio. In the middle of a stream is a pirate ship, and you can go around it in a submarine. You can see sharks. There is a water park, with people lying on a phoney beach in phoney sunlight and swimming in a phoney artificial surf. It all has a distancing effect, so as you walk along the mall, it's almost a comfort to see something you know. "Hey, there's the bank. Gee, the good old bank. Gosh, there's Taco Time. I recognize that."

There's also the killer roller coaster, called the Scream Machine. It's an extraordinary roller coaster. I am a student pilot, but I've never done anything that was as physically shocking as that roller coaster. It's not just terrifying. The G-force this thing puts on your body is so great that when you get off, you say, "Do they have a licence to do that to someone?"

It was very popular until the end of the train derailed three years ago, smashing against one of the stanchions and killing some people. They closed the roller coaster for about two years while they held an extensive inquiry. The final outcome of this investigation was that the coaster opened again and is now more popular than ever.

Go to the mall and get thrilled. Enter the artificial environment. Enter a tunnel of distorted reality. It's quite a wonderful experience the first time. Everything is golden, bright, shiny and light, except for all the discarded human beings who are sitting in the middle of all the noise. These are the farmers who were going about their business on Jasper Avenue when I was a kid but now, in their retirement, are sitting in West Edmonton Mall wearing plastic clothing and wondering where their next piece of human contact is going to come from. Because you can spend the entire day at West Edmonton Mall, and your only communication with another human being will be an economic one. And some very bored teenager will look you in the face and say, "Can I help you?" which means, "Why don't you piss off?" It also means, "Gee, I wish I was somewhere else." And the thrill of the mall wears very thin.

Kenneth Brown, actor, writer and director, Edmonton, Alberta

Gamblers

Our dry, harsh climate dictates that out in the farm grassland area, each farmer needs a lot of space, so indirectly, the climate produces people who are alone. They are independent, they're ornery, they're stubborn. They push themselves, they gamble with the climate, they gamble with everything. And they like to gamble.

If you asked prairie farmers, "Hey, supposing the government paid you an annual guaranteed salary that was easy enough to

Windblown wheat field outside Winnipeg, Manitoba

William McDowell on drought-stricken field, Saskatchewan

live on. How would you like to let the government take the risks?'' they would say no. That risk is half the fun of it; half the fun is getting out there and fighting, pitting yourself against luck, chance, fate and the weather and hoping you're going to make it go. Prairie farmers like to do that. Now, they're shifting into big business, and the kind of personality this business side appeals to may be different, but the small farmer is like that.

Their big gamble is, ''If I'm going to lead a good life, I'm ultimately going to win because God will give me a plentiful harvest.'' So they're usually a conservative, pretty obedient and moral kind of people, but they're gamblers. The gambler does not go out expecting to lose; he expects to win. He'll take all of his risks, and he'll court disaster. Maybe he even likes courting disaster. There's a thunderstorm coming; how is it going to affect me? There's a hailstorm coming; what will it do to my crop? There's no rain; what's going to happen? But he ultimately believes he's going to win.

My dad was a minister, and when I was a kid, I remember some of the questions people discussed. If we've had bad weather all along and on Sunday the crop is in a perfect shape for harvesting, should I harvest it on Sunday? Or shall I wait for Monday, because Sunday is the Lord's day? And there were always farmers who would decide to wait till Monday and risk whatever might happen to their crops in the meantime.

Paul Antrobus, University of Regina, Regina, Saskatchewan

Quinton Pipesteam, Sarcee Nation Powwow, Alberta

Drums

The native people are very rich. I know of those riches; they are not financial. It doesn't matter if my house is falling down or I have to eat bean soup for a week. Anything material can be replaced. But can life be replaced if it's taken away from you?

In the 1960s, we were very angry, out to right all the wrongs white people did to us. But I can't suffer for what is lost and gone. I must now make this place the way we need it to be. I work with the young. I teach the meaning of legends and talk about all the beautiful things the Indian people gave to the Westerners when they came, because the base of our culture is sharing. I do not touch the political side; it's like beating a dead horse.

Yesterday's powwow was a traditional teaching tool. What better way to teach our young about the dignity of our dances and the history of our people? The majority of the dances are intertribal social ceremonies celebrating all people dancing in the circle of life. We dance to give thanks for the gifts the Creator gave us, for our bodies and minds, the sense of hearing and seeing, for being able to dance to the drums that are the heartbeat of our nations. We dance to give thanks for Mother Earth, for the grass we are dancing on, for the water flowing beside us, for the wind that keeps us cool. We teach celebration of those gifts and also respect. After we finish our ceremony, we leave Mother Earth as we have found her.

Linda Boudreau, youth referral worker, Dauphin, Manitoba

Powwow near Dauphin, Manitoba

Women who suffered for that soil

This country was tremendously cruel to women in the early years. They didn't have the opportunity to go out and confront the land and the weather directly and make their peace with it the way men did; instead, they sat inside and got sad. They lived and worked in a very small, constrained space, with the wind everlasting and whistling around the eaves. We talk about the men who tore up the prairie soil, but the people who suffered for that soil were the women.

My mother had nobody to help her. My father was an enlightened man, but he was the son of yeomen farmers in Sweden, where the women worked in the house and the men worked on the land, and if you happened to have five sons and one daughter as he had, that didn't really alter the basic principle; he would

Pearl Ogryzlo, 94, Dauphin, Manitoba

not have thought of sending one of the boys to push the washing machine for her.

Mother was enormously in love with my father. They lived together for 58 years, and I never heard a cross word between them. They started with a sod shack, went through a tremendously difficult first 40 years and put all the children through university. My mother was born in England and came over as a girl with her parents. She was a schoolteacher and a very intellectual woman

Sod-hut interior near Smiley, Saskatchewan

who spoke French and English and learned Swedish after she married my father. For the first 10 years of their marriage, they spoke Swedish at home because my father didn't pick up English very quickly.

She wouldn't have done anything different, yet like most people, she also had to build certain defences. She was a prodigious reader, mostly history and biographies, and I have seen her in the morning kneading bread with the book propped up behind it and still kneading the same bread three hours later, reaching up periodically to turn a page and completely forgetting what she was doing. Later, when my son was a baby, she'd take him in her arms and read until the child would scream in her ear, but she wouldn't even know it. When my parents finally had enough money for train tickets, she would go into Saskatoon, and only a month before she died of a heart attack, she led the discussion on Toynbee's history of England at the University of Saskatchewan Women's Club. Who would expect to find in a house on a prairie hill, seven miles from the nearest town, somebody who has read Toynbee and comprehended the general premises upon which he wrote this historical framework?

Ralph Hedlin, business consultant, Calgary, Alberta

Under the dome

A seemingly disproportionate number of Canadian writers come from the prairies. Maybe they had nothing else to do. But when you go and sit outside between the earth and the stars, you rapidly realize you have to come to grips with something: you're sitting on a bald head, in the middle of a dome, under that sky. It's an extraordinary feeling. Perhaps you also feel alienated, so you value your neighbours a little higher, and you value your inner world a little more.

Kenneth Brown, actor, writer and director, Edmonton, Alberta

Honeymoon

On our honeymoon, he took me to the Great Sand Hills during Christmas. A friend of his had an old farmhouse north of there, and that's where we stayed. There was a windmill and big bins and not much else. We might just as well have stayed outside, it was that cold.

He was so excited to show me the hills. He'd been talking to me about them for two years. ''I have to show you,'' he would say. And he did. I liked the land. We saw some deer, and that was it, but it was nice. Quiet, peaceful. It was pretty to see, even when there was nothing there.

Susan Kenny, nursing student, Winnipeg, Manitoba

Sand-dune patterns, the Great Sand Hills, Saskatchewan

Gold in my hands

Forty years ago, I came from Europe as a farmhand. It was winter, and there was nothing to do on the farm, so I wanted to go to the bush. The farmer who sponsored me said: "You're not a lumberman. They need them stronger and bigger." So I decided to find work in the city. He said: "You go ahead, but if you can't find anything, please come back. We have the food."

I left my wife at the farm and went to Winnipeg with $18 and not a word of English. I was trying not to walk too many streets, scared I might lose myself, and I finally found a church-supply store. I walked in and, not knowing what was appropriate, greeted the owner in German, but he said, "I don't understand." He was a Ukrainian like myself, so our language problem was solved. Then I explained I was looking for work. He showed me reproductions of icons, which were usually just half of a figure of the Blessed Virgin with Christ. He said: "I have customers who would like to have the whole figure. Could you make a drawing of the rest of it?" I said, "Yes, I think so." We went upstairs to his studio, and he made a charcoal drawing and told me to finish it. I did, and he said, "Oh, this looks good," and gave me the painting box with colours and brushes. I worked for one day and a half, and he said: "All right, you have a job. It will be $20 a week." I said, "Wonderful."

I dropped a note to my wife in Saskatchewan and bid her to come. I worked in the store and by chance met a Roman Catholic priest who asked me to see his church. He wanted to redecorate it with some mosaic and ornaments, but I didn't like them, so I asked him, "Could I do my own suggestion?" and he agreed. I made a sketch, and later, he said the bishop liked it. "How much would you want to do the whole job?" I hadn't the slightest idea. It took me almost three months to do the work. One day, he asked me, "Did you ever paint like this?" I said "No." "So how do you know?" I said: "I feel I know. Besides, if you don't like it, I will paint my design over with plain colour and do the ornaments you wanted, all for free." Well, that was fair enough; but when I finished painting the church, he was so pleased, he gave me over $600. I was a rich man.

Another priest came and brought some Ukrainian priests from

Painted Ukrainian Easter eggs

Brandon. They looked at my work. ''Oh, it's so good,'' they said. ''We have just built a church, and it's plain, and we would like it decorated.'' I worked the whole summer there, with two helpers. We painted the walls, the ornaments, the mosaic and the religious images. It was so good, I decided to buy a car. I found a Ukrainian dealer in Brandon, and he started to show me some used cars. I said: ''I don't want a secondhand car. I don't know anything about them, and I can't do any repairs. I would like to buy a new car.'' Then he showed me a two-door Pontiac, and I liked it. It was $2,000, and he said he could arrange a loan. I said, ''I pay cash,'' and he was flabbergasted. But I told him I couldn't buy it unless he taught me to drive, so one of his mechanics showed me all the manipulations.

Next morning, I drove to Winnipeg, parked quietly in front of our rooming house but said nothing about the car. Around noon,

Sculptor Leo Mol in his studio near Winnipeg, Manitoba

my wife said, ''Somebody parked a car in front of the house.'' At that time, there weren't many cars around. I said it was mine. She wouldn't believe me, but later, the car was still there. I said: ''Sure, it will be there. It's my car.'' My wife said: ''Leo, my dad bought a car only after 25 years here in Canada, and you're here just a year and a half, and you have one too. You brought the gold with you.''

And I said: ''Sure. I have it all in my hands. That's all I have.''

Leo Mol, sculptor, painter, Winnipeg, Manitoba

Margaret and I were to be married in November of 1953, but in August, I came down with polio. First, I had a fever. That's all polio is, high fever, and it just gets higher and higher, and nobody can stop it. It doesn't hurt any of the muscles, just works on your spinal cord, killing off the nerves till they stop sending signals, and the muscles just lay there and don't do anything.

They put me in an iron lung, which is like a round bell that pumps air and makes your chest go up and down. I went from about 195 to 90 pounds in six weeks, but I was so weak, I could barely feed myself. If you had just laid your finger on any part of my leg or even my blankets, I'd think you put your whole weight there: the pain was excruciating. It hurt when I turned over and just drove me crazy till everything went numb.

Before I got polio, I drove a cat in the bush, overhauled vehicles and did just about everything. I had also farmed, and after I gained some strength, I wanted to go back to it. I didn't have much left of my muscles because they had deteriorated, but I had some movement in my legs. So I talked to my doctor, who had polio too and was crippled up quite badly. He said he went down to the States to try all these therapies, pools and saunas and ended up spending all the money he had. And he told me: "The doctors will tell you to get therapy, but it does no good to a polio patient whatsoever. Don't listen to their damn crap. Therapists are only capable of building up muscle if you have it. But if you don't, there's nothing they can do." He also said: "If you think you can go back and farm, you're the one who knows that. Don't ask anybody, because they'll give you the rottenest advice. How could they know how you feel?" That was the best advice that I've ever been given.

The first tractor I used was a Ford WD9 with no power steering. If I was to get on it today, I would feel like any other farmer—lost. There was no way on Earth you could move the steering wheel; you had to move the whole tractor. I managed to get around them corners somehow, but I'll never know how. Then I had an old Massey; it steered easier, but it used to turn as far as it would go and lock, so if you made a mistake, you'd go round and round. No wonder there were accidents left and right. The machine companies were awful slow, and it was farmers who eventually invented better things.

The first time I worked the field, I was cultivating. I had lots of field room, and I needed it all because everything seemed to happen so quickly. You generally cultivate angling across the field back and forth, and after a while, you get into the corner and it's all turning. There's little distance, and the corners seem to come fast. That hard steering sure seemed to speed it up, but it was terrific because I could drive and work. What the heck have I been doing, not getting out here before? But after four or five hours, it pretty well had me beat.

Margaret was my legs. To do just about anything, it had to be the two of us. She had to put oil in the tractor, because I couldn't walk around. She had to put the grain in the box, because by the time I did it, it would have been a nightmare. We had seven children, so with babies and diapers, she was pretty busy. She also milked up to 10 cows to put bread and butter on the table.

She did all that before we got up in the morning, and I looked after the kids. She had a built-in radar, and if she figured there was something wrong, she'd come out and help repair things when I had a breakdown. She became a real grease monkey.

There were lots of ways to get me on my tractor, but the most famous and easy one involved my wife. We had a little platform with three steps on it, and I would get on Margaret's back and ride her just like a horse up these steps, then she'd turn around and sit me on the tractor. She said it was twice as easy as anything else we tried. I'm six foot two, but we had lots of fun.

Now, I have a hydraulic lift. If I break down, I radio in for help. My combine has no controls on it at all but a hydrostatic drive, a bit like an automatic in a car. You set the gas throttle in one place, and the engine runs wide open. It also slows it down and speeds it up, and you can bring it to a stop and skid the wheels with the automatic handle. It's very easy to drive. The combine is probably the most advanced of all the farm machines.

It used to surprise everybody when we'd get through the workload the same as everybody else, but I put in lots of 18- and 20-hour days. I remember sitting on my tractor, no cab in them days,

Snow-filled furrows in field near Ravenscrag, Saskatchewan

just breathing the dust right in. I couldn't see my eyeballs through the dust, it was so black. One night, I was out there at about 2 in the morning with the frost on the top of the swath, and I pretty near froze to the bone. Got home about 4 o'clock and was so stiff you'd swear I would crack when I got off that tractor. But by morning, I was right back. I think a fellow has to be a little cracked to be a farmer anyway.

Farming is hard to leave. It draws you. You see the beautiful grass grow and the crops grow and the cattle graze, but that grass and crops and cattle don't always do what you want them to do, so they teach you a lot of patience. I think farmers are probably more patient than most people; they have to be. They wait and watch that crop. One day, a hailstorm comes and knocks the whole crop off, but they're ready to go again next year.

Willard Dow, farmer, Marshall, Saskatchewan

Evening light diffused by rising dust near the Milk River, Alberta

Harvest moon

It wasn't until I came to the prairies that I finally found out what a harvest moon was all about. Sometimes, on one of those days when the sky is hazy and there's still a bit of sunlight left, you may see the moon looming down low just above three combines going across the field and all that dust coming up behind them. The field is so hot, the heat waves are rising, and you see these waves and dust coming up and this big old moon dancing among all that haze. I figure that must be what the harvest moon is, because the field is pure gold, and the haze is gold, and the moon is just floating on a sea of dust.

Randy Hayward, veterinary surgeon, Shoal Lake, Manitoba

The sea of wind

Coming from the East, I didn't know how I would react to the prairie. I ended up loving it. There is a great solitude here, and you can see for such a tremendous distance; you also get little glimpses of things you can remember.

Mornings? I love the mornings. At midday, everything seems to go to sleep because of the impressive heat, but in the morning, the land is alive. You smell the sagebrush, and the air is brilliantly clear and sweet. You don't have the mist you get from the high humidity back East, and you can often smell farms nearby, either the grain or the pasture. There are incredible numbers of wildflowers and birds calling.

When you're out at nighttime, you feel really enclosed because it's so dark. Often, there are no trees around, so you feel like you're in this massive blackness, dark and moist from the dew because it cools down so quickly at night. And that's something you notice too, because you get quite damp. You hear a lot of crickets calling and owls, and occasionally, you sense bats flying overhead. The mice are pretty quiet, but if you lie down, you may feel them running over you. Or a skunk might come along, and you hear him rattling around in the dry leaves. I like to pick up a bit of sagebrush and just crush it and smell it as I walk. Or if the grain is just about right, I pick some of the kernels and chew them, and it's nice. And when the wind is blowing, you get these beautiful wave patterns in the grass: the sea of wind.

Robert Wrigley, biologist, Winnipeg, Manitoba

Talking past each other

I think of myself as a bridge: my wife and children are legally Indians, and I'm the only white person in the family, but most of my life has taken me into the Indian community. Back in the 1950s, I travelled around with my father-in-law to talk to the old people. Now, people say to me: ''You used to talk to my grandfather. Can you tell me what stories he told?'' Because at that time, nobody in the family was interested.

My wife says that in many ways, I think like an Indian, and I know that in certain circumstances, I do. I've learned patience. I've learned to be much more philosophical about accepting things. But the most important thing I've learned is that when something is presented to me that I find curious or unacceptable or irrational, I try to look at it from the perspective of the person who has presented it to me. I've had to do this with Indians all my life.

Let me give you a humorous example. One day, one of our dogs came running to my wife, wagging its tail. She thought it wanted to eat, but it didn't. She thought it wanted to go outside, but it wouldn't go. At this point, my wife became frustrated and said something in Blackfoot that meant, ''If you hadn't eaten shit, you could tell me what you wanted.'' Our dog doesn't go around eating shit, but I understood the situation and simply laughed. In Blackfoot culture, one of the stories is that at one time, the dogs could speak to people. One married woman began an affair with another man, and her own dog became very upset and told the husband. The man beat the wife and warned her never to do it again. The woman took some dog dung and rubbed it in the dog's mouth, saying, ''You'll never speak again, because you gave away my secrets.'' From that time, dogs never spoke. My wife's comment came directly from her culture.

Hugh Dempsey, Glenbow Museum, Calgary, Alberta

Indian elder dancing

of blue. In our spiritual tradition, we also have prints; we call them flags. We go to Riding Mountain National Park, where our grandparents used to live, and hang the flags in a tree. We also take a jar of fruit to share and offer some to Mother Earth. It's a ceremony to let our grandfathers know we're thinking of them. Before we hang our flags, we have to build a little bonfire from fern and sage and cleanse ourselves, but the game warden does not allow us to make open fires. So to do all this, we have to sneak around, and I don't think that's right. I don't think any of us should sneak around in the land of our ancestors.

Julie Cochrane, retired farm worker, Strathclair, Manitoba

Flags and fires

My grandparents lived in Manitoba where Riding Mountain National Park is now, but the park moved them to Elphinstone. Our little reserve was very small, only about three miles this way and four miles that way, and life was very rough.

The children of my mother's generation were taken away and put into boarding schools. If they didn't go, the Indian agent came after them. He would say: ''In school, they'll learn something. We'll teach them how to farm, how to sew and how to wash clothes.'' In the meantime, he would grab little children, the small ones just crying their heads off, and load them in a car. In the boarding school, everything was as different as night and day, and all the white people spoke a language our children didn't understand. Even the white sheets and all these single beds were a fear to them because they had always slept with their sisters or brothers. They were punished for speaking their own language, and when you lose your language, you lose your culture. From that time on, we fall away from the Indian way of life.

But most of us still have our Indian names, and our names usually have colours. My colours are red and black and a little bit

The warmest house in Gimli

When you're used to nailing fish boxes, it doesn't take long to build a house. I did it myself, with no blueprints or anything like that. I was fishing out of Hecla Island in the latter part of the winter, and while I was waiting for my nets to dry, I had nothing to do, so I walked 15 miles to Riverton to get a timber permit. I cut 120 logs, and since I had an old horse, I hauled these logs to the mill a few miles away and worked there for two weeks in exchange for the sawing of the logs. Then I had to haul these 15,000 feet of lumber a mile down to the lake.

One day, a truck with two empty sleighs for hauling fish came along. I asked the driver how much he would charge me for taking my lumber to Hnausa, where I lived. He said, "If you help me load it, I'll do it for $10." It didn't take long to put it on, and he hauled it to the planing mill in Hnausa, where I worked for a couple of weeks again to pay for the planing of my lumber. Then I figured out the size of house I was going to build. We needed two bedrooms, a living room and a kitchen. So I traded some lumber to the harbour co-op for the doors and windows and other stuff I needed. All in all, the house cost me $35.60. I paid that in cash.

Three years later, in 1939, we moved down to Gimli, where I bought a lot for $50. Now, you can't touch them for under $2,000, no matter what kind of a lot it is. A tractor train came along with four sleighs tied together, and I jacked up the house

Soren Tergesen and son, Manitoba

Slough and grasses in autumn, Rolling River, Manitoba

and put it on. We went on the ice for 22 miles and never moved a thing, not even a stick of furniture. Even the cups and saucers stayed in place. My wife was riding inside. Later in the day, we stopped the tractor on the ice and had dinner in the house.

About 4 o'clock, we came to Gimli. I had the foundation all ready, so I drove the tractor in, raised the house off the sleighs, lowered it down onto the foundation, and everything was finished at suppertime. We lived in it for 25 years and then sold it for $10,000 and bought this one. My old house is still standing, and it's the warmest house in Gimli.

It was cheap living for 25 years.

Fred Sigmundson, retired fisherman, Gimli, Manitoba

community life begins to subside and disappear, and you see a lot of children who don't know who their old man is. You also lose all those values that come from stability: friends, family and working at one thing long enough to enjoy it.

When the bust came, there were some real tragedies. There was a guy living nearby who was laid off by Exxon—a geologist, I think. The day after he was laid off, he came home, took an axe to his kid, chopped him up, took a long knife and killed himself too. The fellow next door to us was Chevron's oil-production boss for this area and had been working for that company for

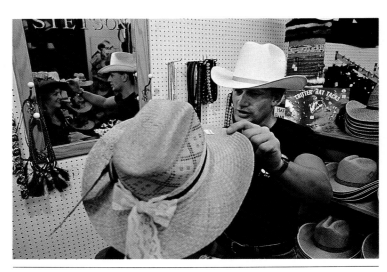

Shopping for hats, Birt Saddlery, Winnipeg, Manitoba

The boom and the bust

Prosperity is a destructive thing. The oil boom spoiled everybody. We all became used to the idea that we could spend every winter in Hawaii, and the fabric of our society began to pull apart very quickly. Every man thought he had to have a girlfriend. We developed a terribly high divorce rate, and many women are trying to raise kids alone. In the past, the idea of family was very strong.

It was not peculiar to Alberta, but any place affected by a boom experiences a tremendous fluidity within its community. You don't know the people living on either side of you because they will only be there for two years, so why get to know them? The

years. He was laid off last month with no warning at all, and he is just beside himself. I think the oil people are not as tough as the old farmers were. When the rain didn't come or when the grasshoppers did, the farmers were used to the idea that they might have one awful year. These guys have had no awful years to get used to.

Alberta has been in a slump for the past several years, and Edmonton has become a very pleasant place to live. There are all kinds of stores with nobody in them. You can drive to work on enormous freeways with hardly any cars, and because you couldn't sell your house this year to get a bigger one, you may even get to know who your neighbour is. A friend of mine said recently, "I've never seen so many bicycles around this place," and it's true. They're having to bring in bicycle bylaws because there are so many people riding them, and they're riding them because they have the time to do it. We can no longer go to Disneyland, so we bike around our town and discover we have a beautiful city. The parks that used to be empty are now crowded with people.

My friends in the oil industry will say I'm wrong, but I think the bust has been a damn good thing.

Ted Byfield, publisher, Edmonton, Alberta

RCMP drill, Regina, Saskatchewan

Creek in autumn, Cypress Hills, Saskatchewan

Earthlings

If one came from outer space to Earth, one would see that this is really a wonderful, wonderful planet with a tremendous diversity of life. But I don't think that such an outer-space being would see man as the only earthling. All other creatures are earthlings as well.

Recently, my cousin burned down a nice poplar bluff that covered about 30 acres, deliberately setting the fire in the hottest days of summer, when all the birds are nesting and all life is teeming. Even though he owns it, I find it totally unacceptable and very symptomatic of our attitude toward the Earth. We decry the burning of the Amazon forests, but we are just as criminal and just as insensitive. We kill the other earthlings, and as we do it, we're committing suicide.

Joe Fafard, artist, Regina, Saskatchewan

Artist Joe Fafard and "Dear Vincent"

Old wolf

They dumped me on a little island on Lake Winnipeg on October 25. It was only about an acre in size, just a place higher than the water so that my feet didn't get wet. I don't think it had a name, just a few shrubs. The day before, I had had some 10 or 12 teeth pulled because I'd had an awful lot of toothaches the winter before, and I wasn't going to go through that again. I didn't want no monkeying around, just wanted to get rid of them. A doctor in Winnipeg did it. I had to pay him a dollar or two a tooth, but it was well worth it.

I had my stuff all packed and ready to go north for the winter in a day or two, but it started snowing and blowing that night, so the skipper had me haul my stuff on the boat. He said, "Let's go before we freeze in."

So we went north, and it was snowing and blowing. At daybreak, we went across and around to the island, and he dumped me there. I had no skiff, just my nets and my sleigh and myself.

And a knocked-down 8-by-10-foot shack that I'd made and could assemble quickly. The skipper rammed the boat as far up on the ice as he could so that I wouldn't have to haul my gear too far, and I carried it all from there up on the shoreline. During the night, my mouth swelled up so much from my pulled teeth and the cold that by the time I had gone ashore to unload my things, I couldn't see through my eyes. I only had one box of aspirins with me, but I piled the net boxes so that I could throw a piece

Painting by Fred Sigmundson

of canvas over them, and that's where I stayed the night—and another and another. I sat there for three days poulticing my face with hot water I heated on the stove under that tarp till the swelling went down and I could see again. Then I built my cabin, and everything was okay. I stayed there from October until March 8, when the tractor came for the fish.

I had no radio, no books, nothing. I knew what the labels on the cans were. I got groceries for $18 for the whole winter. I had some tea and coffee and powdered milk and sugar. I also had a bag of beans and a quarter of a beef, which I paid $2.85 for. Later, I went to the bush and got a deer; the mainland was about three miles in from the island. I ate fish. I was 17 then, and this was the way of life. It didn't bother me. I figured I would make about $300.

I was too tired to dream. I'd get up at 6 o'clock in the morning, walk two or three miles out on the lake, pulling my sleigh and tools, and work all day cutting ice and fishing. Then I'd haul fish back, maybe four or five hundred pounds on the sleigh, get home, pack it all, make myself something to eat and go to sleep. I didn't sing. I may have swore out loud a couple of times, but that's about all. I didn't talk to myself either. I never make any sense when I talk anyhow, so there was no sense talking to a damn fool. Didn't even know when Christmas came and went.

There was an old timber wolf that lived with me on the island. He was just an old fellow, black with a white chest, real nice-looking. He couldn't hunt, so he used to follow me to the net holes and eat fresh tullibees, small fish a bit like herring but worthless to me. He would sit there, tongue hanging out and waiting, while I was pulling the nets. Then he would come along and eat a few fish. I think he had rheumatism or something, because he ran kind of sideways.

He always stayed about two net lengths behind me to make sure the fresh fish were not frozen hard. His teeth weren't that good, I guess. We became good friends. I never bothered him; he never bothered me. I fed him, and he just went and curled up in among the rocks.

He was my only company.

Fred Sigmundson, retired fisherman, Gimli, Manitoba

Being there

There's nothing better than baby calves and colts in the spring and green grass coming and riding after dark and before dark or before daylight. We're still animals; we ain't a machine that goes to bed as soon as you turn it off. Out there, you're close to nature, always thinking about the weather or the livestock and about what to do next and what rewards there will be if you do it good—or what will happen if you don't do it so good. And the rewards, to me, were never money, and I don't suppose they ever will be. The rewards are just being out there, seeing them sunsets like tonight and riding in a snowstorm that most people wouldn't be caught in.

When you ride in a snowstorm, you have to keep your wits about you. It's like trying to ride that wild bucking horse and knowing that if you do something wrong, you could be in really bad shape. You could freeze to death, and that edge makes you think clearly. And you're thinking about where you're heading

Roger Beierbach and his Border collie

Ranch horses on open range, Cypress Hills, Saskatchewan

and where the wind is blowing and about every rock you remember and every fencepost you pass.

You know you didn't just go out there to ride in a snowstorm, but you had a job to do and maybe got caught. But it's kind of neat to see what life is about and how small we are in this world. We're just little, no different than an ant in an anthill.

Roger Beierbach, rancher, Cypress Hills, Saskatchewan

Drought

This summer, everybody has spent more time in this here coffee shop than ever, just to get their minds off the drought. Everything you do costs money, and if we had it, I'm sure we've all got jobs waiting for us on the farm. Most people paint this time of the year, but that takes money too. Nobody's building anything. Chemical and fertilizer sales are way down. The elevators all over are laying people off, trying to figure out how to cut the corners.

Last fall, I seeded to rye, and it came out real good. This spring, it was so dry, it burned right off. It surprised me the crop stuck it out as long as it did; it hung on until last Sunday, and then it started to burn and head out, and that's when you lose your bushels. I knew if I didn't reseed, my land was going to blow away, and we had nine-tenths of an inch of rain on Wednesday,

Norman Tuplin and son inspect drought-stricken wheat field, Beechy, Saskatchewan

so I went and did it; but if I don't get another good shower, I'll have wasted my money and my time. When we get hot wind and loose dirt on top, each shower breaks these little lumps into real fine dust, and the wind just blows it away. That dirt hits small plants almost like a sandblasting action: it sifts across the top of the land and just cuts them off. The plants try to grow again, and another windstorm cuts them off till they die, because they can only take so much.

When it gets that bad, you try to increase your income somehow. I've got into cattle, but it's so dry, I couldn't put them out to grass, and they've been in the feedlot all summer. Other people went to lentils and peas and oil seeds and mustard, things we just don't grow in this country.

One of the biggest things affecting our area is the number of wives who have taken jobs in town. I'd say 80 percent of the wives here are working, but it's killing our town because it doesn't bring young people in. This town needs to keep its numbers up to maintain its water and its sewers, and not many of our kids will stick with the farming.

But there isn't no sense worrying about it. We was born and raised here, and hard times happen. You can't change the weather, so you gotta learn to do everything the best you can and try to make it work. If it doesn't rain, it doesn't rain. And you know, every year, you're going to make mistakes. One year, you seed early, and you're the best farmer in the country. The next year, the guy that seeds late will do well. And so you can be a good farmer or a bad farmer, just depending on what Mother Nature decides. A lot of us say, ''I'm going to start farming on the 10th of May,'' but a few years ago in May, there was a terrible snowstorm, and I had four-foot drifts over what I'd seeded. Others say, ''I'm not seeding until the buds come out,'' but when they come, it might be April or the end of May. The same happens in the fall, and you've got to learn to deal with those frustrations. I find it's better to do something and not sit around, because you can talk about it all the time and just make it worse.

A week of rain here now will be a billion-dollar rain and one hell of a party.

Norman Tuplin, farmer, Beechy, Saskatchewan

Inside grain elevator, Blackie, Alberta

tionships with other women. I hope my daughter won't even have to think about it, that she already has a real caring for herself and a feeling of sharing something with other women, because the world is going to stay patriarchal for quite a long time, and she is going to have to fight that in her life as well. Women of my generation grew up with feminism, so when it hasn't worked, they've blamed themselves: we weren't strong enough;

Keltie

My hopes for my daughter come out of my feeling of inadequacy. I want her to be stronger where I was weaker. More honest. But as a person who has always had to struggle with self-esteem, all I can do is hope that she loves herself.

The more experience I have as a woman living in our society, the more I see it as a patriarchal structure, no matter what we did in the 1960s and the 1970s. We may be able to achieve something, but we always have to achieve it against the odds. We think of ourselves as emancipated and liberal, and we hope our mates are too. But we find that what we're dealing with in our relationships is what our parents and their parents were dealing with. Emancipation is still more of an idea than a reality.

I grew up with boys. There were seven brothers and me, all from various divorces and marriages. My mother always worked, always suffered and always made sure we knew it: a real victim, playing it to the hilt. I rejected it, but I still find myself trapped in the world of men. I'm a designer, but I had to support what my husband was doing rather than what I chose to do. I did the books, the organization, the administration. Wrote up the cheques. I'm trying desperately to start painting again.

There are a lot of very strong women in this community, and for the first time in my life, I've found value and strength in rela-

Selkirk highland dancers perform in Lower Fort Garry National Historic Park, Manitoba

we didn't try hard enough. But perhaps my daughter will have enough sense of self, and it won't cause her a lot of grief. Maybe she'll be able to say, "I want to do this, but I want to do it the way a woman would."

Her name is Keltie. It's an Irish name. It means "kilt weaver."

Heather Redfern, designer, Edmonton, Alberta

Clouds and stones, Coteau Hills, Saskatchewan

New moccasins

Granny Bone doesn't know how old she is, but we think she is 117. She says her mother fell on a stump, broke her back and died; and we're trying to find out how old Granny Bone was when it happened, but she doesn't remember. So we ask her how big she was, but she only says, ''No, I was the same size back then that I am now,'' and she laughs. In the meantime, we know Granny is shrinking, but she doesn't realize she is, so we are laughing too.

When her mother died, Granny's dad moved to another reserve; he died shortly after. It sounds to me that he died from loneliness. Granny says she became very poor because she didn't have parents anymore. Spiritually poor. We remind her she had sisters, but for her, they don't have names anymore. They are just sisters.

I ask her to tell me about when she was a midwife, looking after all these women on the reserve time and time again. She says when the baby wouldn't come, she would wait till the head came out and hold it by the back of the neck and just pull, ever so gently, and tell the mother to bear down. She remembers a lot of the mothers seemed to relax when she'd tell them: "I'm not giving up. I'm helping you."

After the mother had given birth, Granny would prepare a special woman's medicine and give it to her to help her heal inside. I ask what size the babies were, and she says they were all sizes. Some of them were so small, she had to really work on them to get them started. She would cleanse them well with water and wrap them in blankets to keep them warm. Everything was clean, she says, their blankets, clothes, everything. I ask: "What did you ever get in return? Did anybody ever pay you?" And she says: "Oh, yes. They paid me lots. Not in money, but they always gave me something I could use."

She delivered me too. I ask her, "Did you look after my mom when I was born?" She says she did. She says my mom was not sick very long. "Was I noisy?" I ask. "Was I a cranky baby? Did I let the world know I was here?" She says yes, I was very loud. I have to laugh when she tells me that. It just makes me want to hug her and squeeze her because I know we're sharing it, her telling me about my birth.

I remember her setting off as soon as she heard there was a death in a family. She would go with her little bundle of leather and beads and be gone for days. She would wash the body and put clean clothes on it. And make moccasins. We never bury our people barefoot. We must put new moccasins on them—not oxfords or running shoes but moccasins. After you die, you have a long journey ahead of you, and these moccasins have to see you through it. When you get to heaven, it doesn't seem to matter about the rest of your clothes, but you have to have moccasins on your feet.

I'm going to put that in my will. I want a traditional funeral with horses and wagons and people walking behind, and that's the kind I'm going to give Granny when she goes. We've talked about it. She said: "Granddaughter, I don't have to worry. You've made your plans, and that's fine with me."

Mary Bone and Julie Cochrane

Julie Cochrane, retired farm worker, Strathclair, Manitoba

One of the many acts on display at West Edmonton Mall are the Edmonton Oilers practising. It's very much a sideshow. The players skate around, admired by the fans and giving the owners of the mall a terrific boost. Hot hockey on the prairies.

I want to talk about another image of hockey on the prairies. It happened on a family farm, a tiny quarter-section mixed farm, a disappearing phenomenon. The place belonged to family friends called the Clennetts, and one winter, we all went to see them. There was nothing else to do, so the boys cleared off a skating rink on the slough, and both our families, with the exception of my parents and my grandfather, went out to play hockey.

There was a whole range of talent. You had Mrs. Clennett, a sturdy woman in her fifties, playing goal with her galoshes on. And you had old Charlie Clennett, a very wiry, tough little Welsh farmer, and my brother, who was 12 and quite a good athlete, and my other brother, who was 9, and my sister and the three Clennett sons, all big and very rough-and-tumble farm boys, and some of the neighbours as well. I was about 6 years old.

We played hockey in the fading light of an Alberta afternoon until we couldn't see the puck anymore. It was challenging and tough. I was playing with big, strong men who didn't mind knocking me down if I got in their way; that was farm life. But I had more finesse because I had had more free time to skate on

.

better ice than they had, so I was able to skate around them sometimes. And we had Mrs. Clennett, bawling instructions to her kids, and Mr. Clennett, this wonderful, wiry old man, who has since died of cancer, playing not a bad game. There were no nets, so people made goals with their boots, and the actual count of goals was extremely irrelevant, but I've never had a better hockey game in my life.

Somewhere between that slough and the hockey shrine of the Edmonton Oilers lies Canada's fascination with the game. Cana-

Snow blowing on open prairie near West Bend, Saskatchewan

dians think if we can still beat the Russians on the ice, they won't invade. And there's nothing that can arouse Canadian passion more than hockey, because it's the only thing that every Canadian can look at and say, ''Yes, that's something we do distinctly as a nation, and we do it better than anybody else.'' Because what the bloody hell do you do for six months of the year when you don't have West Edmonton Mall or swimming pools and your television is a sort of grey? Almost every Canadian male who grew up on the prairies or came from that ethos played hockey and in some part of his psyche believes he is scoring the winning goal in these games.

Since then, I've written *Life After Hockey*, a play about a man who believes he scored the winning goal in a major Canada-Russia hockey game. The power of the play is in those universal memories of what it feels like to be a 6-year-old skating.

Kenneth Brown, actor, writer and director, Edmonton, Alberta

Britany and Arnold Elliott feeding newborn calf, Smiley, Saskatchewan

On night call

I came here five weeks ago as a new graduate to work at the clinic, and my very first case was a bag of dead chickens. The farmer wanted to know why they died. I love horses—they really dragged me into veterinary medicine—but poultry doesn't interest me. So I looked at these dead chickens and didn't want to do it at all. It wasn't hard to diagnose, just a case of intestinal parasite, very common on the farms around here. But there was such irony—to come here all keyed up to look after horses and get a bag of dead chickens.

My greatest fear was a Caesarean section on a cow. In college, they expose you to as much as they can, but that was one thing I hadn't done much on my own. I thought maybe on my first couple of cases, Bruce, the clinic's owner, would show me what he does, but the first one came during my night on call, so I had to go by myself. I didn't know the roads, and I had to do an operation I had never done in the farthest corner of the practice where I had never been. It was nighttime, so I couldn't find any landmarks. All the red barns and the second signposts on the left disappeared.

When the farmer had called me, I asked him: "Do you have power in case I've got to use clippers? Have you got lights tied up someplace for us to work with?" And he said, "No problem, no problem." When I got to the farm, he had the hood of his Ford truck on the ground with the heifer lying on it. He didn't have a trailer, and because the heifer was lying on the ground and he couldn't get her up, he rolled her onto the lid of the truck and hauled it up to the house with the tractor, with two chains hooked onto the hood. He had her under a dim yard lamp, with mosquitoes as thick as could be, and for a surgery light, he produced an old lamp with a bulb in it. When he held it down, it shone more in my eyes than it did in the womb.

My experience that night was one of the best things for my confidence. I managed to find the cow in the dark, on roads I didn't know. I got the calf out, and it was alive. The mother lived. They got no infections, and I did it all by myself. After that, everything's been easy.

Arnold Elliott delivering a calf, Smiley, Saskatchewan

Randy Hayward, veterinary surgeon, Shoal Lake, Manitoba

A wild place

It was more than 20 miles to town. In those days, you just didn't drive that far, so we had to find something else to do. It was nature we looked to; it affected our whole life.

We were always rafting. The water was full of bugs, frogs, toads, salamanders and snakes, but of all our pets, the toads were the best. They were brown with red spots and a little yellow on the belly. We'd feed them ants and grasshoppers, and their tongues would fly out. They had trouble eating ants, though: they would tear them off their tongues with their hands, sort of irritated by them.

We kept the toads in a big square metal tub. We'd put in some dug-up sod, tip one side up and pour water in the lower end, so they had a pond and could also go into this sod with tall prairie grass. If the water dried up, they'd all dig into the soil and disappear. We would look in that tub and wonder if they'd got out on us, but as soon as we'd sprinkle the soil with water, they would start popping out and this old tub would become a wild place.

Dean Francis, artist, Mantario, Saskatchewan

Porcupine on road, Big Muddy Badlands, Saskatchewan

Red fox running on open prairie near Eatonia, Saskatchewan

Running away

How often do you see wildlife in the woods? Very seldom. You see the occasional bird or a deer, but it's just a fleeting glimpse unless you're lucky. But out on the prairie, animals have adapted over millions of years, and now they know it's inefficient to run away unless they have to. Watch the mule deer. When you startle them, they'll run a bit and then turn around and have a look at you. There's no point in running away from something that can't catch you. So they'll just stand there, and after a while, they'll start grazing. The sharp-tailed grouse will do the same— fly up the hill, turn around and look. And the jackrabbit.

Here, you only run long enough to be out of danger. Then you take a good look, and if all is well, you just take care of your business.

Raymond Kenny, biologist, teacher, Winnipeg, Manitoba

the right way, it works. And if you practise it in love, it always works. We've been living it for 450 years.

We fear that if we send our children to school in town, we will lose them. You know how children are: the weak ones join with the crowd, and away they go. That's why we bring the teacher from town to teach our kids right here in the colony. You can't bend a tree when it's fully grown, and you can't teach a child something when he's already a teenager.

The government we had before this one really didn't like the Hutterites, and the educators in Alberta knew that if they could

A fence around a garden

We say that in a Hutterite colony, all people are taken care of from the womb to the tomb. The security of the community is tremendous. I'm not saying the whole world should live like this, but if it did, there would be no mental institutions, no old folks' homes. If every community would care for their old, their sick and their mentally handicapped, the government would save billions of dollars.

What we're striving for is to love our fellow man and to be happy. Any wrong done among us is to be forgiven and forgotten; otherwise, the colony will break up. We didn't invent the communal system; it was invented by Jesus himself. Of all the flowers and the fruits, he talked about the grape because they all grow together. Of all the animals, he talked about the sheep because they all live together. And of all the birds, he talked about the dove because they all flock together. If one flies by itself, the hawk will get it. That is what he believed, and if you practise it get our children to school in town, we'd lose them and the communities would slowly fall apart. They tried to bus our kids, but we wouldn't allow it. The worst thing in town is drugs among teenagers, and we were scared some of our children would get involved. We protect them.

We put our children to work in the colony when they are 15, and that's when their education really begins. We have just built a hog barn, one of the most modern in Canada, all computerized. Our veterinarian teaches the kids about the pigs, and my son, who is 20, will be the pig man of that barn. But we don't rush our kids to mature and leave us. My daughter Rosa is 25 and doesn't have a boyfriend, but I never thought she should look for one. I keep telling her, "Your mother was 28 when she got married, and you got lots of time." Then she tells me, "How come you got married when you were 21?" And I joke, "I didn't want your mother to become 35."

At harvesttime, I think about old age. You plant those little seeds in the spring, and then you go out and reap what you've sown. You can't expect wheat if you planted wild oats, and if you don't plant good seed in your children, they can't produce what you had hoped for. We put a fence around our children like around a garden. You water the seed, you hoe the seed, but if you don't put a fence around it, who will walk in? The sheep and the goats, and pretty soon, there will be nothing there.

Michael Gross, Pincher Creek Hutterian Brethren Colony, Alberta

Sunrise Hutterite Colony, Hussar, Alberta

Demolished grain elevator, Golden Prairie, Saskatchewan

Dying town

At one time, this used to be a hopping little community. But now, the hotel's been moved out, and the grocery store has been torn down. There is no more post office or blacksmith, and this may be the first summer ever they are not going to have church services here: it costs too much money to have the church open.

Those few people who still live here are all retired farmers. Home is home, and where else can they go? A farmer has a different outlook on life than people who are mobile, and a lot of them have never been more than 70 miles away from home. When retirement comes, you'd think they would move to Vancouver, but no. They've never seen anywhere else, and the fear of the unknown looks after them.

Farmers have always been independent, and they don't need a lot because they grew up without very much. When they come to old age, they don't need the luxury of someone looking after them or the convenience of good stores and fresh fruit. They've done without it all their life, and they don't need it now.

Ian McPhadden, farmer, Milden, Saskatchewan

Too long in the sun

You can live a very placid and boring existence in the prairies, and many people do. And yet our fiction is populated with crank characters, people who lived here a little too long and who have been out in the sun a little too much. They have crazy ideas, like building a boat in the middle of Saskatchewan to sail it back to the homeland in Scandinavia. And there is Saint Sammy, a prairie prophet from the novel by W.O. Mitchell, who lives in a sod hut, eats locusts and is almost biblical in his eccentricities.

If you want to be different, there's room for that. Maybe because the prairies are big, and maybe because our communities seem to tolerate their eccentrics very well. But when you hear about the scandals going on in these small towns, you realize that they're not nearly as upright and benign as they appear to be.

Jars Balan, poet, writer, teacher, Edmonton, Alberta

Having a wonderful time

I love to see little boys with turbans playing hockey in the street. To me, this is just what Canada is all about. Nothing makes me happier than to ride a bus and hear three different languages. I remember once walking through a shopping centre and seeing a very old Filipino woman pushing her cart with what must have been her great-grandson skipping along and chanting a jingle from the McDonald's commercial. The woman was probably born in a hut somewhere on an island, and the child beside her most likely spoke some Spanish but also knew English, and they were both having a wonderful time.

Philippe Mailhot, curator, Winnipeg, Manitoba

Chinese dancers at Folklorama

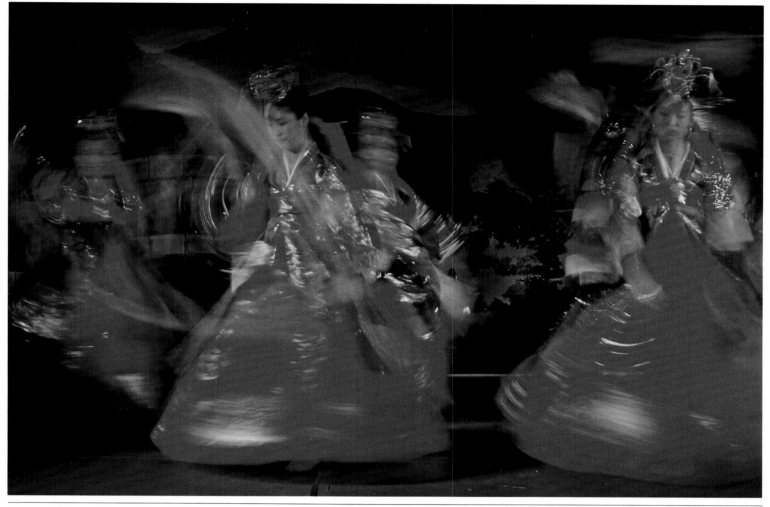

Korean dancers performing during Folklorama, Winnipeg, Manitoba

We danced together

I'm 83, and I had the good and the bad all my life. The good was raising five sons and the pleasure of a wonderful wife. She was one of the best that God should have ever given me. She was a wonderful mother with her children. She was a great person with all her neighbours. She was a hell of a good cook, and when I'd be riding a bronc that was hard to keep away from barbed-wire fences, she'd get on her horse and crowd between me and the fences so I didn't get hurt. And she helped me many times when I'd get bucked off and get a really bad break.

She made things beautiful. She was my greatest little gardener, and she raised one of the best gardens along the creek. She raised corn and beans; she had squash and potatoes and small cucumbers. She'd take a baby out in a big box with a mosquito netting on it and work in the garden so we'd have something for the winter. She raised flowers, every kind—geraniums and pansies and roses. That was out of my line, but I loved them the way she did. She also taught my kids to believe in God. She was Roman Catholic, which I was not, but I was satisfied she was on the right road.

She had a mind that was wonderful. Oh, she read an awful lot. She'd read a book in one night and tell me everything that was in it. She had an excellent memory. I'd say, "Do you have any idea, honey, where I put the part I wanted for that old car?" and she'd find it for me, sure as the world. She also made an awful lot of clothes, and she could patch stuff you'd think was past patching and make it last another few days.

She never hunted, but she knew how to care for what I killed. If I got a deer or antelope, we'd pull our meat up high on the der-

rick away from the flies, and it would hang there in the breeze all night. In the morning, we'd let it down, cut the meat off the bone, put it in jars and sink them in a cold, shady spring that boiled continuously. She had a string tied to them to pull them out when we wanted some fresh cold meat.

And she could make a hell of a good antelope steak on an old wood stove. One time, I shot one over the hill, in line with a large

Howard Buchanan, Saskatchewan

hay derrick to make sure I didn't hit anybody in the yard. But when I came in, she said, ''Howard, you shot the house.'' I said she'd just heard the echo over the hill. ''No sir,'' she said. ''You shot the house.'' So I started to look along the wall, where I had put tar paper and some banking of dirt. The house wasn't much, just a dirt roof and a few ply boards with a lot of paper in between for insulation. Finally, I found a little hole, so I went inside, and she smiled and said, ''Now, are you satisfied?'' ''Yes,'' I said, ''but where do you suppose the bullet is?'' And she took it out of the arm of the chesterfield. She could've been sitting there, and that bullet could've hit her.

We danced together, we rode together, we travelled together in an old buckboard, a two-wheel cart I used to break broncs, with her in the box, holding the kids. We had 51 years together before she passed away six years ago last March. She had a bad heart. But there are very, very few that you hear or see today that could do the things that little girl could do. Yes, she sang, she danced, she rode horseback. She kept busy at all times.

She's done it all.

Howard Buchanan, retired rancher, Consul, Saskatchewan

Grainfields, the Wintering Hills, Alberta

Lots of it

I'll tell you a little story. My son-in-law came down here a few years ago, and he had never been on the prairies before. I went down to Regina to pick him up, and after we got out of town, I told Bill, "Take a look to the north while we're on this level land." And he looked for a moment and asked: "What's out there? What is there to look at?" I said, "Take a look to the south," and he did and said the same thing. "Now," I said, "this is what I like about the prairies. There's not a hell of a lot to see, but you can see lots of it." He agreed this was okay, but he preferred mountainous country. I like the prairies better. About a month ago, I went to Olympia, Washington, and it's a beautiful place with lots of trees, a pretty bay and big mountains. But I didn't like that country. The scenery went by too fast.

Jack Pye, retired railroad engineer, Moose Jaw, Saskatchewan

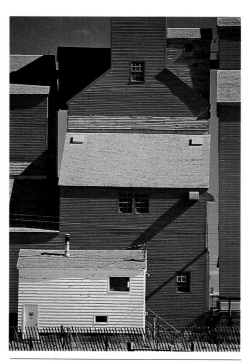

Grain elevator, Saskatchewan

Linda Elliott and son Kelson, Smiley, Saskatchewan

Together

I am never bored. I can be with Arnold all the time, and he discusses everything with me. If we're sitting down at the table and talking farming things, we have to do it over the noise of the children. Every morning, he gets up and says, "We've got to achieve this today," and I have to work it into my schedule. I never have all my washing or all my dishes done, because he comes in and wants me to go to get parts or drive the truck over here or hold this nut so he can screw it on. I love it. When we first started to farm together, we couldn't put our hands on enough money for collateral to buy this land. It was like a wilderness, and nobody wanted to put a road up here. For five years, we worked for his father for $1 an hour. Dad would get us up in the morning as if we were children and have us running the tractors for 12 hours a day or more. But we always dreamed and designed our house on paper till we came here and built it.

We work together under real stressful conditions. Sometimes, we're all uptight: the combine is taken apart in the field, and we can't find this nut and bolt in the dark, but we must fix the machine so it can go again at daylight. He's yelling at me, and I just take it in stride, because I know he's under stress; so I just stand there and try to do everything he's saying. But when I'm under stress, he understands it too, and there is never a problem, because we can talk together.

Linda Elliott, farmer, Smiley, Saskatchewan

Autumn patterns in freshly harvested grainfields near Drumheller, Alberta

Whenever a white person spoke, I used to jump. Didn't matter if it was a white child or a white lady: I was scared. I knew loneliness. I knew how to live in fear. To shy away from people. I was warned: "If you ever talk about this, you'll get more and worse." But what more and worse could I get?

I was 3 years old when my mother died. She was behind the curtain on a homemade bed, and I wanted to lie down with her, but I didn't know she was ill. Somebody kept taking me out of there, but I kept going back until I heard some old people crying. I didn't know why they cried until I lost a friend, a boy who had been like a brother. We were running on a cold winter day, and suddenly, he bled from the mouth and was smothered to death. I went to his funeral, and something dawned in my mind; it was as though my mother were being buried with that boy.

After that, I was sent to Elkhorn, Manitoba, to a boarding school run by an Anglican mission. I remember my grandfather putting me on a horse wagon and saying in our language, "You're going away," and that's all I can hear today. In school, everybody was warned not to speak our Indian language, but the day came when I had been caught too many times speaking it, and I was punished. That was in 1928. Later, I wrote that number wherever I went—in the barn, in the dirt and even on the rock—1928. Why? It is a mystery to me.

The person who punished me was an Anglican missionary. He was slapping my face left and right, saying: "Jesus Christ died for you. Your people are savages. You're no good." My tender face was red-hot, but I didn't cry. I couldn't understand why he was hitting me. Weren't there any other boys to be punished? Weren't there any other girls to be punished? Why did it have to be me? Then he asked me to take off my clothing, which was just a piece of coveralls, and he smacked me once on the rear. I burst out crying. I filled his room with my cry. I begged him not to hit me anymore, but he strapped my hands behind my back, tied my ankles and put me on a high stool. After he left, I fell off that stool, and by the time he woke me up, I'd messed up the floor. He spanked me again and ordered me to get lukewarm water, cut a big bar of soap in half and stir it in that water. And then

Young dancers at Alberta powwow

he said, "Wash your mouth with it." In a short time, my mouth was raw. My nostrils had soap coming out. I thought I was going to die of thirst.

Then he put me in an empty room. I was as lonely as can be, crying and crying, then I couldn't feel anything. Later, the same man came back. He brought out his penis, but I was 5, and I didn't know what he meant, so he shoved it into me, and I fainted. I

didn't know when he was gone. I tried to get up, and I couldn't, because he hurt me. Then I said to myself again: "Why? That's the man saying, 'Jesus loves you.' What am I supposed to believe? That people are cruel and I have to be scared of them?" It was a long time before my spirit was healed. Before my body was healed. Before I could eat. Before I could play. Even with my fellow Indians, I was afraid. I was afraid of life.

When I was 13, my father took me out of school. I began to listen to my elders telling me how my ancestors had suffered, how they died like flies, how bounties were put on their heads. And everything came back to me. It was because of my language, my colour, my culture. "Aha," I thought to myself, "this is why I was punished."

And here I am today, 60 years later, and it isn't much different. Racism is in the papers every day; it's like cancer, and you can't cure it. I call it Canadian stigma: it's made in Canada, and I meet it everywhere I go.

Gilbert Abraham, certified orderly, Winnipeg, Manitoba

Topsoil blowing during sandstorm near Hanley, Saskatchewan

A prairie rainstorm with a little dirt in it

If we didn't have a car when that storm caught up with us today, you'd have to pull your shirt over your head or lie down and put your nose into your garments to try to filter out some of the dust. Otherwise, you'd just about suffocate. When a rainstorm like this happens, it usually storms in the upper atmosphere and a weather front is moving through. That white layer above the field was a hail shelf: it forms when the rain starts to come down, and the atmosphere storm sucks it up and makes ice. Until it all begins to churn, you're okay, but when it starts to roll inside, that means it's getting ready to let go of that hail. Today, you saw a prairie rainstorm with a little dirt in it, a partial tornado or hurricane, and we only hit the edge of that moving dust wall because the rest of it went west. It's hard to say how many miles away that dust is coming from; it just rolls and rolls and blankets everything, closing you right out of the sunlight. It's called a blackout. In the 1930s, they used to set the cups and plates upside down on the table to keep the dust out till you were ready to eat.

One tornado we had blew stuff in all directions. We had a 28-by-60-foot barn, and its metal roof lifted off and scattered over 3½ sections of land; some pieces went south, some went east, and some went northeast. One big rafter flew through a narrow space between the disc and the packer and went straight into the ground with such tremendous force that we had to use a front-end loader to haul it up.

Some of the whirlwinds are just miniature tornadoes, and we had them just about as bad this year as in any of them. There are hundreds of them in the spring, and the bigger ones take you right off your feet. Once, I was trying to fence and had to quit; my eyes got so full of dirt, I had to feel my way down the road. But I was raised in this country, so it wasn't difficult.

Elmer Sira, farmer, Hanley, Saskatchewan

Prairie travellers near Hanna, Alberta

Rituals

Food is very important to keep the culture alive, just like music. It is a part of a ritual that binds people together. When somebody moves into a new house, I always bring along a loaf of bread, a bottle of red wine and a piece of cured or smoked red meat. The wine is for good health, the bread so you'll never be hungry, and the meat is so you may prosper. I don't bring money but something that nourishes and lets us carry on.

Such rituals give us a sense of belonging, of believing in something. They build memories for old age and help our grandchildren to remember. On Christmas Eve, we always have the traditional Ukrainian dinner with the 12 meatless dishes, and my children and grandchildren wouldn't dare eat anything else. They wait for this ritual all year: "Oh boy, we're going to Baba's; we're going to have fish; we're going to have prune dumplings." They really care, and it gives the young ones a memory to fall back on in times of stress. The child who has no memory or tradition has no sense of direction and is totally lost. "Who cares for me?" he asks. But if he knows Baba cares and mother cares and somebody else cares, he feels strong.

Traditional dishes require a lot of effort. That's just the way it is. Once you care, other people will too; it's a two-way street. It doesn't matter whether you give attention to food or to those around you or to material things; it all matters. Because if you take care of your shoes, they'll be all right for a while. But if you just throw them in the mud, that's exactly what you're going to have: a muddy pair of shoes.

Marion Staff, owner of Alycia's Restaurant, Winnipeg, Manitoba

Tom Francis and grandson

Elmer Laird cooking breakfast pancakes, Davidson, Saskatchewan

Dishwasher salmon

I'm game to try anything that's easy and sure-fire, because my cooking is a little haphazard and the seasoning is never the same way twice. I never measure; it just depends on what I have on hand. Never a great disaster, but some meals are better than others.

To make sure that it's not overdone, I cook my fish in the dishwasher, and it comes out the same way every time. A friend mentioned it to me, and I tried it. It worked, so I've used it ever since. You take a whole fish, clean it, stuff it, wrap it well in double aluminum foil, put it on the top rack of your dishwasher and run it through a normal cycle. When the cycle of washing and drying is through, your fish is done just right. And it's always the same, because the heat and the timing are identical.

It's just wonderful for salmon.

Edith Landy, retired nurse, Winnipeg, Manitoba

Farm buildings and abandoned wagon, Hazlet, Saskatchewan

It's funny how we change

I remember we came to the prairies on the last day of December. I didn't want to go to Canada, but I had no choice. Well, I had a choice. I could have left my husband and stayed behind, but I didn't want to leave him. A farmer sponsored us, and we were to stay with him. They brought a taxi and covers of all sorts, wrapped me in all that and took me to the farm. It was dead winter, 40 below, and I couldn't even breathe. When we were leaving Holland, it was plus 17 degrees Celsius, and I carried a huge bouquet of my own chrysanthemums aboard the train.

The country was so desolate, so empty. Even when we came to Winnipeg, the first thing I said was: ''Oh, Leo, where did you bring me? It is just a big village.'' Coming from Holland, it was a big village.

It's funny how we change. At first, I would come home and cry, the people seemed so strange to me. It wasn't what I was used to. Everybody was so indifferent; they never asked any questions. And then the years went by, and one day, someone asked me about something, and I said: ''Leo, why should they ask me that? It's none of their business.'' Then I laughed and said, ''Do you remember how I used to come home and cry that no one was interested or willing to associate with me?''

One year, we went back to Holland. So many people; it's just awful how crowded it is. Now, I don't like going to Europe; it's too congested for me. But I love driving through the prairie here. I don't care where I'm going and how long I'm going to stay. I'm ready to go anytime.

Margareth Mol, teacher, Winnipeg, Manitoba

Darlene Stacheruk, Saskatchewan

That scared me

I got sprayed with grasshopper poison last year. The line blew, so I had to wait to pump the tank off before I could drive my truck home, and my whole body got sprayed. I got home dizzy and scared and yelled at Dad to read the instructions on the pail while I just hit the shower, soaking myself down and washing; but he ran in, yelling, "Don't use soap! It drives this particular chemical into your skin." We took the name off the label, went to Kindersley Hospital, 30 miles away, and the doctor said, "We can't give you an antidote unless you're within minutes of dying, because it's almost as bad as the chemical and could make you terribly sick."

I came home all weak. I lost the use of my arms for a while and couldn't control the muscles; they were gone. That scared me. I had real thick, curly hair, but suddenly, it was turning grey, and some patches were falling out. I slept a lot and became very passive. Even now, I doze off quickly, and my muscle power isn't coming back.

The grasshopper poison attacks your nervous system. They told me that from now on, any chemical will affect me, but it's pretty hard not to be exposed to them. This year, I was back spraying again, but I think we should be growing less grain with more weeds in it and simply cleaning it properly. If you're getting a decent price for your grain and you know it's chemical-free, you don't have to grow that much, do you? But they're spraying by air, they're spraying the ground, and the air has just reeked of chemicals the whole last month. Our rivers are polluted, our lakes are polluted, and the chemicals affect many farmers, but we don't look far enough into the future.

Arnold Elliott, farmer, Smiley, Saskatchewan

Arnold Elliott and newborn calf

Cattle and riders during autumn cattle roundup, Cypress Hills, Saskatchewan

On the trail during wagon-train outing near Tulliby Lake, Alberta

Cross country

I have a team of horses and a covered wagon. We get together, maybe 30 wagons and 100 outriders, and just go across country the way they did in the old days.

Last time, we went early in June. The first morning, the four wagons ahead of us stopped at not a very appropriate place, because the lady from the *Western Producer* magazine wanted to photograph them on the incline. The wagonmaster was trying to get them going, but I was caught halfway up the hill, and my team, still cold after the night, couldn't hold the load. I lost my momentum, my brakes seized, and the wagon went down to the river backwards, falling straight over a 15-foot drop and into 4 feet of water. The wagon box floated down with my wife inside, but we were lucky nobody was killed. We salvaged the wagon, and I made the track the rest of the day, but none of my family wanted to ride with me. We lost our luggage, our food, and we couldn't even have an open fire because the summer had been so dry.

The next morning, everybody was still very upset, but you can't worry long doing something like that. Almost every wagon train has somebody musically inclined, so in the evening, you have a singsong, and you visit all day with other people. It's

Allan Brown, wagon-train master

really pretty out there, lots of grass and wide-open spaces. No fences. And you can touch on some historic spots and still see the ruts in the ground and tepee rings that hadn't been disturbed and places where a stagecoach used to run and old sod barns.

We sit in the wagon and ride all day; then at night, it takes a whole family to put a camp together, unhook the team, drive the pegs in the ground and help with the supper. We have all this time to talk to each other, and suddenly, we are not rushing anywhere.

Norman Tuplin, farmer, Beechy, Saskatchewan

It's hard to say "I love you" to your child if you've never experienced love yourself. My father was an alcoholic, and I thought if I was like him, he'd love me.

But you don't find yourself in a bottle. You become a person of many masks. I've been in community development since 1968, when radicalism and alcohol were accepted as tools. I also married an alcoholic and experienced a lot of violence. My eyes were swollen shut, and my nose was spread across my face; it'll never heal. For 19 years, I wandered what we call the dark road, with alcohol, drugs, anger and jealousy. Then I began to look at my four children, and I thought they deserved better than that. So I quit. I didn't know my gifts, my strengths or my weaknesses until I became sober and entered the cultural way of my people. No one can exist without a belief in a power greater than himself. That's why we wander on those dark roads.

If I were rich enough to have grandparents, they would have taught me about my role and responsibility as an Indian woman. Women are the ones who carry children, who carry life in the water from which everything living comes. We are the teachers. But when I decided to turn my life around, I didn't know who I was. I became suicidal because I thought I'd been abandoned, but it was I who abandoned myself. To be a total person, I had to understand the four faculties I had: the physical, emotional, spiritual and intellectual. I also had to heal within, cleansing all the bitterness and hatred toward people who have harmed me. I had to put into myself things like love, kindness, honesty and sharing.

I began to examine my heritage. My father is a Cree Indian, and my mother is Scots and English. When I found my Indian name, I knew what I had been running from all my life. It was as though I was relieved of a large burden, and I began to really grow.

Drinking is a symptom of many things, but I don't believe our people suffer from an identity crisis; they suffer from the absence of a positive identity. There's a real spiritual revival going on across the nation, and it's beautiful to see. The children are thirsty. They learn about themselves. They start to understand that sweet grass represents Mother Earth's hair, and when you

Youth in front of bar, Alberta

use it, you purify yourself. They see we're all equal, down to the smallest child and the oldest person.

We were all given gifts. Some people are artists, some are dancers or writers, but everybody has something special. If we take just the four of us here, put our four gifts together and decide to do something, there is no way to stop us. We all know what we are good at, so we'd have it done in no time. That's how it works, even down to the smallest child. And among these children, I'm no more the teacher than they are.

Linda Boudreau, youth referral worker, Dauphin, Manitoba

Slow recovery

Today, I know more Indians who are reformed alcoholics than ever before, and there are more successful programmes that usually combine Alcoholics Anonymous and traditional cultural practices. My closest friend was a skid-row bum in Calgary for 10 years. One morning, he woke up in an alley as usual, pulled a cardboard box off his body, sat up and said to himself, ''Pete, what are you trying to do, kill yourself?'' He went into a programme twice, hasn't had a drink since and, until his health prevented him, was the alcoholism counsellor on the reserve. Once people do become dry, they often want to help others. But recovery is very, very slow, and a great many Indians completely lose themselves in alcohol. The young ones start sniffing gasoline when they are 7 or 8, then move to glue and start drinking when they're 13 or 14, so by the time they're 16, many are confirmed alcoholics.

Hugh Dempsey, Glenbow Museum, Calgary, Alberta

Old photograph

Prairie history is still so close, you can touch it. I like going through old cemeteries because when you learn to read the tombstones, you find incredible stories. You see whole families that died in the influenza epidemic or in a fire, because fires were so common in the pioneer days. You see how many people died in the spring, and you know they must have had a very long and hard winter.

The dates and the words are hints. I remember looking at the tombstones near Dauphin of five children who had all died within a year of being born. When you looked at the dates, you could see their mother must have been pregnant whenever it was physically possible. One child was born in June 1922 and died in March 1923, and another was born in March 1923 and died in September 1923. And the irony: she named her last child Vera, which means Faith. You stop and think: What is it for a woman to bury five of her children?

On Saturday, I went to see the grave of a couple I love to visit. He was in the Austro-Hungarian army, and after he died, a little building with a peaked roof, door and window was built between his tombstone and his wife's. When you look inside this strange little hut, you expect to see an icon or pictures of both of them, but instead, there is a picture of the Austro-Hungarian royal family, and you wonder why it was so important to him. And you'll never know.

I like driving the back roads of the original Ukrainian settlement because those places are rich with associations to me, and my ethnic kinsmen give me a feeling of ownership. One day, I was passing through the town of Wostok, the second oldest Ukrainian settlement in Canada, and I found a little tavern, not much bigger than a living room. Inside, there were four or five farmers talking in Ukrainian, so I asked them where the oldest cemetery was. I explained I was writing a book on Ukrainians in Canada and could he tell me where, for instance, the old Nemirsky homestead was. Right away, he looked at me sharply and said, "Nemirsky? How did you know my name?" I told him I had a book with a picture of the first Easter service on the Nemirsky homestead, taken in Wostok in 1898.

Tombstone and old photograph

And since I happened to have the book with me, I showed it to him. He became very upset. He said the caption read it was the home of Andrew Nemirsky, but that wasn't true. It was his father's house, not his uncle's. ''Who told you this?'' he demanded. He blamed me for the mistake. And I thought: Here we are, discussing this photograph taken in 1898, and he's telling me he grew up in that house and the book is wrong. And I thought about other people whose lives and work we use to study the history of the prairie, and yet we can still meet their relatives and associates who could tell us about them. What were they like? Did they have a sense of humour? Did they have a temper?

Jars Balan, poet, writer, teacher, Edmonton, Alberta

Good Friday procession, Ukrainian Catholic church, Model Farm, Saskatchewan

Rustling

I was already raising cattle when I got married in 1930. Then we tried to raise grain on the creeks, where we could get a little water. One year, we'd have an exceptionally good crop, but the next year would be no good for anything. This is what we call a sunny desert.

But it has been a hell of a good area, with not much rustling ever. We heard 'em talk about it in different places—rustling, rustling—but hell, it's just talk. These cows are just like human beings: an odd one dies, some disappear, some fall in beaver holes along these creeks, and you'll never know where they went. They're just missing, and if it was a small animal, coyotes would eat it in a week. So we never accuse anybody of rustling. In the earlier days, if they had positive proof, they didn't go to too many courts. They just took the guy out and threatened to hang him.

Howard Buchanan, retired rancher, Consul, Saskatchewan

Ranchers roping calf, Cypress Hills, Saskatchewan

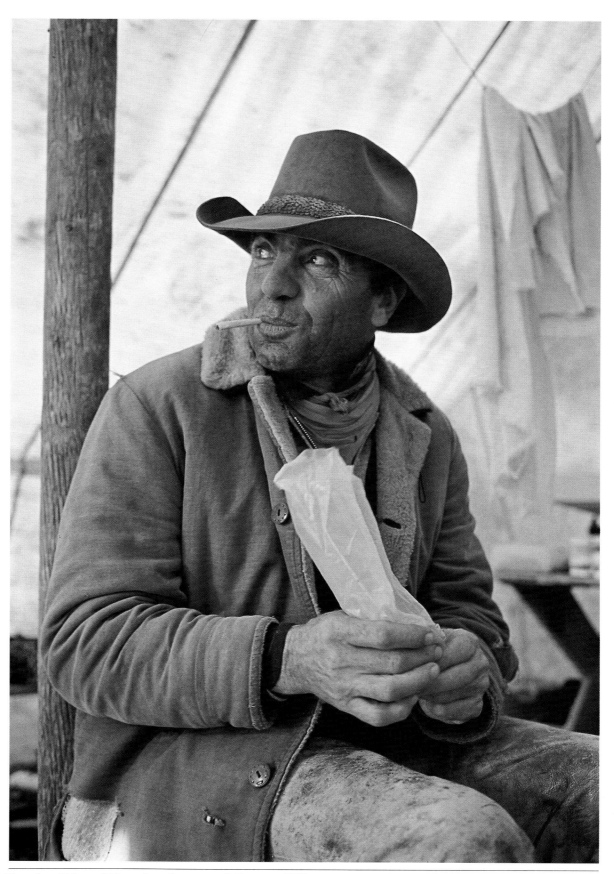

Rancher Edward Nuttal at the annual Cypress Hills autumn cattle roundup, Saskatchewan

Coyote, Cypress Hills, Saskatchewan

Coyotes

Coyotes are clever animals, or they wouldn't be around. Man has waged war against them for so many years, poisoning, shooting and trapping them, and still, they hold their ground. They don't like the farm dog very well, so they lure him away if they can and attack him. We were haying this one year, and our dog, a big Alsatian, had gone with us. All of a sudden, I saw this thin, bedraggled old coyote walking right close to us. I thought, "Oh my goodness, that poor thing is half-starved." I knew as soon as our Pal sees it, there was going to be a big chase, and sure enough, the dog spied it and just swished after that coyote. They both disappeared over the hill, but in two seconds, Pal came back a lot faster than he went, with three coyotes right after him; the first one lured him to where the others were waiting. Pal was really pouring on the coal to get away from them until he jumped on the back of our half-ton truck, where he was safe.

Marjorie Robinson, retired farmer, Saskatoon, Saskatchewan

Burrowing owl at sunset, Moose Jaw, Saskatchewan

Farmer's lung

Spraying chemicals on the farm is terribly hard on the health, and grasshopper spray is the worst. I'm wondering in my own mind if this buildup of chemicals isn't going to do us in someday. People die from it, and we farmers probably use it more than anybody else. To top that off, 10 years ago, I got into a bin of grain that wasn't dry enough. I was shovelling the spoiled stuff from the top and all the time breathing in this real bad dust that sifts off rotten grain. It got into my lungs and just about finished me.

You're always in dust out here, but years ago, we never thought about that. I rode on open tractors for years, and it didn't seem to bother me; but now it does, even when my wife sweeps the basement floor and the dust comes through the ventilating system. My lungs probably got so much dust over the years that they're all plugged up. They call it farmer's lung.

Norman Tuplin, farmer, Beechy, Saskatchewan

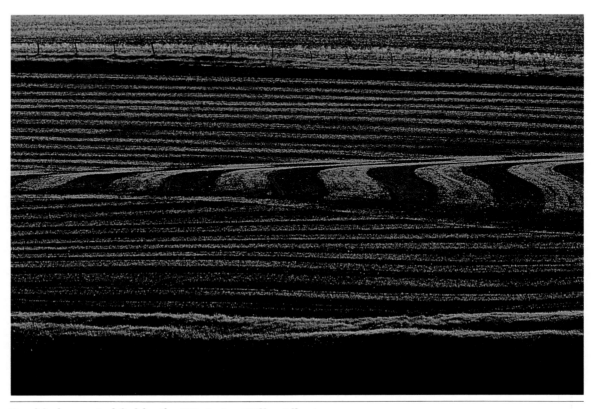

Freshly harvested fields, the Wintering Hills, Alberta

Stubborn

Do you know that an average North American consumes 8½ pounds of chemical additives every year? We seldom question the need for them.

Farmers believe chemicals are necessary to increase the productivity of the land; they also use them because the industries that sell those chemicals have very good marketing psychol-

Gerald Norek working his field, Gerald, Saskatchewan

ogists whose ads are designed to appeal to the farmers' self-interest and to manipulate them into believing they cannot do without them.

I talked to one stubborn farmer who survived the 1930s in southern Saskatchewan. Three years ago, we had a huge grasshopper infestation. His neighbours on all sides used chemicals, and the next spring, they had little grasshoppers all over their property. This guy refused to spray, but after the grasshoppers had laid their egg sacs in the ground, he went out with a harrow and, without turning the soil over, just made a slice underneath, breaking 90 percent of the egg pouches. I walked across his land, and there were almost no grasshoppers there at all.

Paul Antrobus, University of Regina, Regina, Saskatchewan

Let's have a picnic

There's no way to live on these prairies without being cooperative. The weather is so relentless that you need your neighbours in order to survive. People develop a great number of co-ops and other self-help structures. I remember many examples of such cooperation; one took place in the little town of Shellbrook, where people wanted a new skating rink. That was par for the course: a town of 2,000 needed a $400,000 rink, which would be a million dollars now. They had no money, but that was no problem. There were some make-work programmes for the winter, so the farmers went down to Regina to get a timber permit. They cut it, hauled it out, got somebody to saw it up, piled it out for a season and let it dry. They also needed some cash, so they set up a little co-op, worked on it, got paid for it in make-work project grants, signed their cheques back, and pretty soon, they had the rink.

And that's how small Saskatchewan operates. Farmers are very handy people; they've got machinery and know how to use it. They also know how to go about things, and it's absolutely a treat to deal with them. If they decide they need something, they call a meeting and get everybody committed to the project.

I remember one CCF picnic. Good, we'll have a picnic; but what do we need? We'll need some seats, because we'll have speeches; so you'll get the barrels, and I'll go over to the co-op and borrow the 2-by-10s, and we'll just set them up and later take them back. Now, what about the mosquitoes? Right, done; I'll bring my spray machine, and we'll buy a pound or two of spray, and I'll spray the trees. How about something for the kids? I know someone who has some ponies. I'll go down and borrow his po-

Townspeople watching softball game, Mossbank, Saskatchewan

nies and bring them up here—great fun for the kids. And in about 20 minutes, everybody knew what to do.

They're all entrepreneurs with a tremendous sense of community. It's less so now, as they become more of the TV generation and think the world is like *Miami Vice*, but that sense is still very true in rural Saskatchewan, and it will arise again in times of adversity.

Allan Blakeney, former premier, Regina, Saskatchewan

From the underbelly of the dream

During the great oil boom, Edmonton was a very strange and ugly city, filled with young men making very high wages and driving very large 4 x 4 trucks. Those young men have now gone back to where they came from because the money has dried up.

At first, there was a sense of astonishment about that new wealth. As late as the early 1970s, Edmonton was a hick town, with people in dirty, grubby farmers' clothes walking around downtown on Saturday afternoons and getting their shopping done. Then they were suddenly bumped into this cosmopolitan world where their social life was no longer just a matter of church on Sunday and where all their solid, stolid, post-Depression values were quickly put under assault by the massive incursion of new ideas, new people and new money.

I would occasionally drive a cab in the summer, and I'd pick

Moon and downtown Calgary, Alberta

up these men who had just flown down from the oil fields with $2,000 in their pocket and wanted to know where they could find a woman. Ten years ago, it would have been indecent to ask a cabdriver here, ''Take me to where I can find a whore,'' although it was done in Toronto or New York or Chicago. But it was a bush mentality, and Edmonton was investing in that mentality with a lot of glitter.

Edmonton rose to their expectations. It literally rose. If you looked across this river valley when I grew up, you could see three prominent features: the Alberta Hotel, the golden dome of the Greek Orthodox church and the Parliament. Now those features are obliterated by the soaring glass towers built during the late 1960s and in the 1970s to serve someone's dream about what a city should be.

I'll tell you a story from the underbelly of that dream. Our cab company used to take the calls no one else would touch. One night, I was sitting in the bar in the York Hotel and got a call to go up to Dickensfield, one of the brand-new subdivisions built literally in months. The sewers would be put in one day, the light fixtures would go in on the second, and all the foundations would be laid on the third. It was just massive construction on a scale I don't think very many places in the world have seen.

I went to Dickensfield, found the address and knocked on the door. A very worn-out West Indian woman came out with a half-naked East Indian guy. After some unsuccessful bargaining, he finally threw her out with a five-dollar bill in her hand. She staggered down the stairs, incoherently drunk. I helped her into the cab and drove her back down to the York Hotel. The five dollars was the fare down. She offered to have me take up the fare in trade, which I declined, so she staggered out of my cab and into the York Hotel to try her luck again.

I will never forget the expressions on the faces of those two people. He was East Indian, and she was West Indian, and the irony of this encapsulation of the boom was not lost on me a bit. For her, being picked up by some poor, desperate East Indian guy that night was her share of the wealth. For him, that was his share of the wealth too.

Kenneth Brown, actor, writer and director, Edmonton, Alberta

Going crazy

I come from New Brunswick, and to me, everything here is new. I have to feel my way around, but when people give directions, nobody says "Turn right" or "Turn left." They say, "Go a few miles north, then east and west." Everybody lives by the compass because the roads go north, south, east and west, and all the dirt farm roads are laid on a grid unless there happens to be a lake they have to go around. Between each section, there is a right-of-way, and there are roads down the edge of farms from driving equipment up and down. Sometimes I look at a map, and I think how much farmland is lost underneath all that asphalt and gravel which never grew there before.

Back in New Brunswick, my parents would drive 90 miles to see me at the university and stay overnight before going home, but out in the prairie, 90 miles is something you do in the morning. When we went back East for our honeymoon, my wife, who comes from Saskatchewan, looked at the map and picked three little towns she wanted to visit. And I said, "That's all you want to see?" She said, "Yes, that's enough for one day." It was a small stretch, but she was used to prairie distances between three towns, which could be a day's drive. Back East, the towns are so crowded, there's hardly any space between them. My whole hometown could easily fit on any farmer's field out here.

Everything in the prairie is on a large scale. In the fall of the year, you can watch combines going all day, going all night, going all tomorrow, just running full-bore. They've got to get that crop in when it's ready, and they've got to get around that rain. You can feel the tension. Everything's buzzing. The equipment dealers stay open 24 hours a day repairing machines, because farmers won't ask, "Well, can you get my thing fixed on Wednesday?" If it's broken today, it's got to be running tomorrow. But back in the Maritimes, a guy works away with his little tractor, and if he blows a bearing, he drives to town, where he might

Billboard near Vanguard, Saskatchewan

Wheat field, Pincher Creek, Alberta

get the part or maybe just spend the afternoon visiting. It's not a big deal.

Here, it's big business, and the pressures are tremendous. Just a few people are putting in an awful lot of crop, and if they're using big machines and a lot of technology, one man can do an awful pile of work. But he also has no time to look at his livestock, and some animals that come to our clinic during harvest and planting time are in very poor shape. And it's not the farmer's fault. He can't be everywhere. He's running his tractor until the sun goes down and for a long time afterward, and he's got to eat and sleep sometime.

One morning at 3 o'clock, I was driving to do a Caesarean section on a cow. And everywhere I looked, there were headlights, farmers just going crazy all over the fields, working. They had a dry spell with more rain coming. They had to get their crop planted. They had to race against the clock and the weather.

Randy Hayward, veterinary surgeon, Shoal Lake, Manitoba

To ride a bronc

I began to rodeo when I was 15, but I roped goats and calves when I was younger than that. We fixed a milk cow with an old saddle, and this old roan cow would buck. Then I started to ride broncs. In those days, the horses were wilder 'cause there were a lot more fresh ones, and they would be kicking and snorting and flipping over. I was always skinned up. There were other guys shaking like a leaf, but I was never scared. I was crunched a time or two, but I got over it quick. I just got bigger and better, and the horses got better and tougher.

To ride a bronc, you kinda lift your reins in front of you, and that sets you down. Your feet go over the point of the shoulder, and you've got to hold them there for one jump. I'd let my feet hang straight down and then throw 'em over and right forward, spurring the horse's shoulder or neck, where the points and the money was. The higher in the neck you spur, the less power the horse has. And then you try to get in a rhythm, just like dancing, because you can't overpower a 1,400-pound horse. One time in Calgary, this old stock contractor said, "Let's see some mane in your rowels when you get back." He figured this horse, Moody River, would buck me off, because she did throw a lot of guys. But when I came back and showed him the mane hair tangled in the rowels of my spurs, he was as happy as I was.

When the rodeo season started, we would all jump in one pickup and head down the road. We'd put 1,000 miles on my brand new Chev in one night and sell it before it was a year old with 100,000 miles on it, just from rodeoing. In the 1970s, a lot of the guys were rig rats from Alberta who had a little money, and gas was cheaper. Sometimes we'd all stop at our ranch, get a bath, and Ma would cook us a big old steak. A lot of other guys could do anything between carpentry and oil rigging, but they didn't have a home.

On the road, you saw some awful tough cowboys too, driving terrible wrecks; it ain't a quitter's sport. It's jarring to your bones, and that striving to be number one and all that driving burn you out. But if you get hurt, everybody helps. I've seen a fellow with his arm broken and hanging at the elbow, and everybody was there to get him going again. It's like on-the-road correspon-

Swift Current Rodeo, Saskatchewan

thinking about irrigating your field when you are in the middle of a bucking horse, you ain't gonna do it.

There's no better feeling than being a rodeo cowboy. It gets in your blood, and you can't get it out. You miss the people but also the competition between you and the horse. Man against beast, like gladiators in Rome, I suppose.

It's a great life, but you just don't last forever, and that's what's wrong with it.

Roger Beierbach, rancher, Cypress Hills, Saskatchewan

dence: you learn as you go, and the guys tell you everything they know, as if saying, "Try to beat me, even if you know my secrets." I've got nothing but good to say about it. I think everyone should go rodeoing; then it would be a lot better world.

You had a dance at every rodeo, and if the local guys were gonna beat up some cowboy, the cowboys hung together, and it would be a free-for-all for a while. But mostly, people enjoyed seeing the rodeo in town, especially in farm communities. I think a cowboy has always been the top of the agricultural list of jobs.

But in the end, I got a wife and two kids and had to make the ranch bigger if it was going to go on. There would be no place to go when you got old, even if you won all those championships. A rodeo cowboy was never a heavy-working man. Rather, he was allergic to work, or felt he was.

So I went back to the ranch. But in mid-March, I'd wake up in the middle of the night with that spring fever. I'd have nightmares about going to a rodeo, but there is no in-between. If you want to go and win, you have to stay in shape; and if you start

Rodeo cowboy, Swift Current, Saskatchewan

141

Kerchiefs and ribbons

Hutterite women can't partake in meetings and are not allowed to decorate themselves with any kind of frill. When I came to visit the colony, I had my hair braided with a ribbon, and I looked like a Martian to them.

Since the men were having a meeting, the girls took me upstairs. They knew me already, so they immediately asked me to braid their hair and put ribbons in it, but only for a moment, just

Girls watching calf roping, Pincher Creek Hutterian Brethren Colony, Alberta

to see what it all looked like. They had no ribbons, but they went and cut strips from fabric their mothers had saved for something else. They brought some flowers, and I sat for about two hours braiding the hair of all 10 of them. French braiding, all the way down their backs. Then we put flowers and ribbons in. They were all so beautiful.

That weekend, they had other visitors too, some boys from a colony in New York. It was a matchmaking encounter. The boys heard there was something going on upstairs and came up to see what the excitement was all about. They caught the girls looking as they've never looked before, and all I heard was: ''Sarah, you look gorgeous'' or ''Elizabeth, you are beautiful. I didn't know you looked like this.'' Well, they didn't even know what these girls looked like under those polka-dot kerchiefs.

Then their father came upstairs, and he couldn't believe it. They were gorgeous. He was the head of the colony and didn't know what to say, except for ''Yes, you all look very nice, but don't do it again.'' The girls felt so badly. It took us so long to decorate them with this beautiful hair. So they asked, ''Can we leave it like this?'' and he said, ''Yes, but you have to put on the kerchief.''

So the braids stayed, the kerchiefs went back on, and everything was hidden again.

Irka Balan, choreographer, Winnipeg, Manitoba

Great Grey Owl, Winnipeg, Manitoba

Playing a flute in the Great Sand Hills

One year, I lived in a tent in the Great Sand Hills. When I stayed for the winter to study kangaroo rats, the locals thought I was pretty strange. And there was no way around it; it was bloody cold. There wasn't enough snow to make a snow hut because a good snowfall there is only two inches. There was no shelter from the wind because there are no trees. Good thing I had a German shepherd willing to crawl into my sleeping bag.

Picture a gerbil, only a time and a half larger, light brown on the back and white on the underside, hopping on its hind legs and really cute: that's a kangaroo rat. Their tails are long like on a glider, and the whole musculature in their hind legs is much like a spring, storing energy with every bounce. Because they can aim themselves with their tails, it's very difficult for a fox or a coyote or a hawk or an owl to catch them. They can jump straight up several feet and literally reverse their direction 180 degrees without losing speed, leaving their predators confused. I know firsthand that when you jump to catch them, you just end up with a fistful of sand.

I would often stay up at night and play my flute. I don't play it very well, but I guess the sound was unusual and peaceful

Mule deer, South Saskatchewan River Valley

enough for the animals, and they would come. First the deer, then the coyotes, literally within a few metres. They were curious, but I was in the dark, and they were in the moonlight and couldn't see me. They would listen and walk around until one of them would catch my scent and bolt. I wouldn't see them again that night, but sometimes, from the next field, the coyotes would howl back.

Raymond Kenny, biologist, teacher, Winnipeg, Manitoba

Somebody else is going to save the West

Westerners are certainly being made to feel different. We are Canadians, but most of our people are not British; they came from Poland and the Ukraine and many other places. They don't have a great connection with the British Crown, and they also have this ferocious American influence because of the oil industry. There's no deep commitment to Canada here; it's a superficial thing, and the loyalty to the province exceeds the loyalty to the federal government. And once the government is established in the minds of most citizens as something that's somebody else's and not theirs, then you have a dangerous situation. It sits waiting for some explosion to occur, and it has been badly handled. Trudeau said, "I saved Quebec, but somebody else is going to have to save the West," and that may be true.

Ted Byfield, publisher, Edmonton, Alberta

You take care of us

During the war, I was in an infantry battalion with a lot of Canadian Indians. They were very good soldiers, and we used to always be together. There were no groups, white or red. It was assumed that after the war, they would move into white society and simply get jobs, but it didn't happen. They all went back to their reserves, which was really tragic because there was no wilderness economy to support them. Many are now on welfare, and there is no hope at all.

My Indian friend told me once, "When the buffalo disappeared, God gave us the white man, and now, you guys will have to look after us forever." He has a great sense of humour, but there is a terrible feeling of guilt in our society and not a single way to resolve the problem.

Eric Wells, news commentator, Winnipeg, Manitoba

Bull bison on Schmalzbauer Buffalo Range, Hoosier, Saskatchewan

Pesticide-container collection site, Olds, Alberta

Our own mess

We are the only farmers in our area that haven't sprayed for about 17 years. Everybody else does. They spray for bugs. They spray for weeds. They spray strawberries to make them red. They spray lettuce to make it crisp. And they laugh at us. I say, "Laugh all you want; I want to live long enough to get my old-age-pension cheque."

At first, we didn't tell anybody we weren't spraying, because it wasn't the thing to do. Then last year, people were complaining they couldn't meet their expenses, and I said, "We didn't spray, and we didn't use fertilizers, and we made money." And I told somebody who was bragging he had already spent $12,000 on spray, "I wouldn't brag about spending that kind of money on stuff that isn't good for you."

The television is always advertising: "You've got to use this and this and that." Older farmers are more careful, but the young people are ready to use everything they're bombarded with, and some who had their land given to them by their fathers don't have much respect for the soil. They want to get big quick, but it doesn't work that way.

People are beginning to worry. Most women read and hear more than men do, and a lot of them want their husbands to stop using chemicals, but the husbands say, "I can't farm without spray." It's not that they can't—they're afraid to try, and unless the consumers say, "We do not want polluted food," the spraying will go on, because some farmers just don't care. They take all they can out of the soil as quickly as possible, but 20 years down the road, that soil won't be producing like it is today. Everything on this Earth is for us to use properly, and if we make a mess of it, then it's our mess.

Violet Kasper, farmer, Colonsay, Saskatchewan

Field of rapeseed, Mannville, Alberta

I'm sure happy I didn't leave

My husband never really said what he expected of me. Our first child was born nine months and 18 days after we were married, and it was pretty rough, because I didn't know how to cook, and I didn't know anything about the farm. We had no running water, no toilet, and the diapers froze in the pail on the bedroom floor. And I knew nothing about babies.

Our daughter was born in the summertime, which is the busy time of the year for farmers. My husband was happy because he was building me a cistern for running water, but he had all of these people helping him two days after I came home with the baby. I was trying to nurse, and I really had never had that many people to feed before. I had taken out a package of hamburger meat, and the baby was colicky and screaming, and I was supposed to look after her as well. That was the most crushing thing.

After that, it got worse. Our crop that year was almost a disaster. We had nothing but rain. Rain, rain, rain. We harvested our

Sky at sunset, Manitoba

150

flax in December. I was so happy it rained, I didn't even feel guilty, because my husband was home with me and our little girl instead of out on the field. It was also hard because I had grown up in a very unhappy family. My mother was sick all the time. There were six of us. We were very, very poor, and I mean poor. My father thought he would end up farming, but he never, ever did make it. My mother had a nervous breakdown and was gone for a year and a half. I was 12 years old, the oldest girl, and I looked after the family.

My school was a release. I was out of prison when I went to school. The first day I went there, I found that letters made words, and the words were like a great big door to the whole world. I read all the books I could lay my hands on. That was also my undoing, because I read escapist literature. I would read anything that had a happy ending. Even when I went to teachers college, I was still dreaming, thinking, ''Here's this wonderful man I've fallen in love with, and we are going to move to the farm, and everything will be roses, a happily-ever-after ending.'' But there just wasn't one. I wanted to be a writer, I wanted to be an opera singer, I wanted to be a nurse, but I just saw myself having one baby and then another baby and another.

He was happy. He's always been very earthy. He had a good childhood and a large family. But I kept reading this escapist literature even after we were married. I was very insecure, and if he looked at anybody who was pretty, I was jealous. If it happened nowadays, I probably would've left, because now they make leaving seem so easy. It takes some people a long time to grow up. But I did, sort of, and I'm sure happy; I'm sure thankful I didn't leave.

I was extremely lucky. Another man probably wouldn't have put up with that. He was very patient. He was more mature and waited for me to catch up. He was a farmer, and I had gone to teachers college, so I thought I knew more than he did. But most education doesn't come out of books, and he knew a lot more than I did. One thing I regret is that I didn't give my love of reading to my children, but I was scared they would end up trying to escape the way I did.

Betty Schlichting, farmer, Sanford, Manitoba

Empty gravel road at sunset near Acadia Valley, Alberta

Across the border

During Prohibition, people came from Montana night and day to buy liquor. They forgot about the border pretty much, and many of the trails they used didn't pass the customs house at all. After a while, the ruts got so deep, they looked like cow trails. The cars were the Fords and the Essex and the Studebakers, and they had high wheels with wood spokes. They had radiators on them, but water was the only thing we knew in those days. Some tried to mix coal oil with it and use it as antifreeze, but they weren't too successful.

When my wife was to have her first baby, I took her 50 miles south to our closest doctor in Havre, Montana, and left her there. Then a wire came saying she had gone to the hospital. The snow was about a foot and a half deep, so I saddled a horse and led one to ride later. About halfway, I changed horses and turned the other one loose. I rode into Havre and tied my horse to a telephone pole at the Grey Nuns' hospital and learned I had a boy. But to get home, we had to take the train from Havre west up to Coutts and Lethbridge and then to Manyberries and to Govenlock on nothing more than a freight train with a caboose hooked on. It took us three days.

Many times, we had trouble getting any help. One day, my mother haemorrhaged, and I brought her an old doctor who'd been in the war. He was shell-shocked and in bad shape, but I dragged him here, all wrapped up in fur coats, first on a saddle horse, then on a sleigh. When I unwrapped him at the house, he said, "Is there any place I can lie down for a few minutes?" And I said, "By God, I didn't bring you here to sleep but to save my mother." And he did that very thing.

One time, we went shooting big white jackrabbits on the ice here. They were jumping on the bank to get away from us, so I took my gun by the barrel to pull one down. By the time I shot again, the end of the barrel had frozen over, and the extractor on my .22 blew out and went right into my eye. The only place to go was Havre in Montana, but I had an old T Ford, so the family bundled me up, covered the one eye, and I had to drive. They also took two saddle horses just in case. The snow was about nine inches deep and very loose, but we went down the old trails until we got on the American side. Our method of moving was pretty crude: we had to pour water into the old T when it boiled from fighting the snowbanks, and we also had to keep it from freezing by pulling a blanket over the radiator. I ruined my sheepskin coat because I put it over too, and the heat blistered it all up.

Later, I got the part of the shell taken out of my eye, and I could see the same day. I'm going blind now but not due to that old damage. The doctors say it's hardening of the arteries behind the eyes. They give me two years.

Howard Buchanan, retired rancher, Consul, Saskatchewan

And the desert will bloom

I started reporting during the Depression. I was working for a paper that was Conservative right to the core, and for my first political story, I was sent to cover a press conference put on by the Liberal Member of Parliament. While we stood in his office, the dust was blowing all over the prairie, and he went over to the window and drew the word "dam" in the dust. And he said: "If the Liberal government is reelected, we'll build the South Saskatchewan dam. We'll irrigate the plains, and the desert will bloom like the Garden of Eden."

I was only 18, a young kid on a first political story, so I went back and wrote that the desert is going to bloom if the Liberals are elected. Then I handed my story in and could hardly wait to see my big story on page one. I was having lunch in a Chinese restaurant when the paper arrived. I looked through it and couldn't find my story at all. I went through the front page again, and then I saw my byline. But instead of the blossoming desert, the story by Eric Wells was about the biggest Liberal bribe ever offered to the electorate by a Member of Parliament. It mentioned the Garden of Eden, but it also reminded the reader about a serpent in the Garden.

I thought a terrible thing had been done to me, and I was determined to resign. The phone rang, and it was the Member of Parliament, who said, "Mr. Wells, I want you to come over right away." I rehearsed what I'd tell him: "Sir, I've resigned. I wouldn't have anything to do with such a rag." But as I walked in, he stood up and held out his hand. Then he said: "I didn't know you were that smart. That's real political reporting, and I wish we had somebody on our side who could do it. You're going to go a long way in this game." So I didn't tell him I hadn't written it. I took all the glory, and later, he offered me a job.

I went back to my editor all confused, and I asked him who had

The Great Sand Hills, Saskatchewan

rewritten it. He said he had. He said, "You're new to this game, but the Liberals have promised to build the Saskatchewan dam at least five times, and whenever they're in trouble, that's what they do." I asked, "Is that how you wanted me to write the story?" "No," he said, "you're a reporter. I want you to tell the facts; but I'm the editor, and I tell the truth." And it's something I've always remembered: there's a big difference between fact and truth.

Eric Wells, news commentator, Winnipeg, Manitoba

Snow geese during autumn migration, Teo Lakes, Saskatchewan

Imitation French Quarter in West Edmonton Mall, Alberta

A million stars

In 1987, 17,000 people left Saskatchewan farms and moved to the cities. The year before, it was 25,000. Now, farmers constitute only about 18 percent of the population. A lot of this is a result of farm foreclosure and the economic situation, but as people move away from the country, they become isolated from the elements that used to rule their lives.

When you live on the farm, you can't walk from the farmhouse to the barn without seeing a million stars. Two or three hundred nights of the year you see a million stars every time you go outside at night. But in the city, you cut yourself off from the most reliable indicators of the infinity of nature. The sun isn't important because you can manipulate light and darkness with artificial lights. Your air conditioning and heating can manipulate the seasons too.

On the farm, you drill your well, and you're always aware of the water level. In the city, you turn the tap on until city council says, "Sorry, no more water for your lawn, we haven't got enough." But do you realize that the water-table level on a farm five miles out of town has been going down for the past 30 years because the city has been sucking it in for its people?

You turn on your tap and drink the water. But the native up North says: "Hey, 30 years ago, I used to catch fish out here, and they were beautiful and vibrant, and the water sparkled. We enjoyed eating the fish, and we were healthy. Now, the water is yellow, the fish are discoloured and not as active, but we've still got to eat them, and we don't feel so good."

But when you get your crystal-clear water from the tap, you don't notice anything. Our artificially constructed environment separates us from the consequences of our own behaviour. We have this stupid illusion that as long as we don't see these consequences, they aren't real and we don't have to worry about them. Then suddenly, we learn the ozone layer has holes in it. We learn about AIDS. But where do we go from here? Are we going to create synthesized natural settings?

We're here because our parents survived to childbearing age by knowing what to do. But we've been cutting ourselves off from the information we need to keep surviving—from the weather, from day and night cycles, even from temperature. The only time we come in contact with nature is when a tornado, a cyclone or an earthquake smashes our house apart. But those are pretty rare.

Our bodies developed over millions of years in response to nature, and we used their warning signals to tell us what to do. Today, we can ignore them for a longer time, just as we ignore a pain until it becomes a cancer. But if we weren't able to air-condition, to manipulate the light and darkness and control bugs and the air with all kinds of sprays, we would be in a natural setting and we'd recognize change a lot sooner. People have been talking about the destruction of our lakes and trees and soil and air for 40 years. But those who are making the decisions live in sheltered, artificially constructed environments, and they don't really see anything.

Paul Antrobus, University of Regina, Regina, Saskatchewan

Dominick Krupnik, Manitoba

Louise Big Plume near Calgary, Alberta

Havens for Indians

The Plains Indians have developed a culture based in all its aspects on the buffalo, but the Europeans dispossessed them of their land and destroyed the buffalo. On the Canadian prairies, this process occurred rather late: the disappearance of the buffalo began in the 1840s, but it wasn't until the 1870s that it began to affect the Indians. By that time, the government of Canada had developed an attitude based upon an earlier edict of King George III that the Indians should be recognized as the occupiers of their land and that they could surrender it only to the government, which, in 1870, suddenly found itself with a vast, open prairie, a commitment to build a transcontinental railway and a great number of Indian tribes to deal with.

Over the next seven years, the government negotiated treaties with each of the tribes, signing the last one with the Blackfoot in 1877. The Indians gave up their rights to the land and in turn were given reserves and other amenities, such as agricultural tools, hunting and fishing equipment and the right to get educated. At the same time, their entire economic base, the buffalo, had been eliminated.

The reserves were initially perceived to be havens for the Indians, and the land was provided on the basis of five people per square mile. In more settled parts of Canada during the pre-machine age, a family could do quite well farming a quarter section of land, so giving a family of five a whole section looked as though it were a generous settlement that would allow the Indians to become self-supporting.

But they had no history of farming and no leanings toward agriculture at all. Their whole way of life had been completely destroyed. The government initially anticipated it would take two years to transform these buffalo hunters into farmers. Then it became 10 years. Then the date became indefinite. During that time, the government issued rations of beef and flour as a temporary measure to keep the Indians alive, but soon, these rations became a weapon. If Indians were wandering into towns and cities or were becoming uncooperative, their rations could be cut.

It also meant that if an Indian stayed on his reserve and didn't do anything wrong, getting rations was no longer a temporary

Sandhill cranes during autumn migration, the Great Sand Hills, Saskatchewan

privilege but a right. There were no long-term plans for having the Indians develop as farmers, and although there were individual successes, the general agricultural programme of the Department of Indian Affairs was a failure. The Indians became Canada's first people on permanent welfare.

Hugh Dempsey, Glenbow Museum, Calgary, Alberta

even a bit late, she would stand at the door with her hands on her hips, screaming at the top of her lungs, ''You naughty little faggot! You know you're late,'' while I was still a block away. She used to call me that because I was very thin. I don't know who was more scared—the rickshaw driver or me. Then I would have to play scales and Bach, and she'd be chain-smoking and breathing all this smoke at me. I'd come home all covered in ashes and crying. It was not a positive learning experience.

But I'm grateful to my parents, who always encouraged us to use our minds. There was no television in our home until I was

I am doing what I want

I began to sing before I learned to speak. My mother used to sing to me, and since the Mennonites are great ones for breaking into harmony, I heard four-part harmony in church all the time. Our farm was famous for its huge yellow-tiled silo. It could be seen from miles around, and when it was empty, I used to ride my tricycle inside it and sing. The echo was phenomenal. I was 3 years old, and all I knew were hymns, so I belted them out in this great chamber.

I was still a child when my father took up the oboe. At the beginning, the sounds he made were horrendous. They sounded like the mating call of some long-extinct bird, probably of the duck family. Those initial attempts were so painful to the dog's ears that when it was hot and my father would play on the porch, we'd hear his terrible oboe sounds and the dog's howls. It used to drive us crazy, but he stuck with it and became a very accomplished oboist and English horn player. He taught voice and learned to teach flute and clarinet.

He wanted me to be a cellist, but I was a small, skinny kid, and you can't imagine how much I hated that huge beast: I would have made kindling out of it at a moment's notice. We went to live in India for three years, and I had to take lessons with the principal cellist of the Calcutta Symphony. She was an Englishwoman with flaming red hair and red fingernails, and she had a very, very British accent. Every day, I had to get into a rickshaw with my cello so my driver could pedal me to the lessons. If I was

21, and we grew up learning. We read, we played games, we did puzzles and had to use our imaginations. When we returned to Canada, my father said: "Whatever you do, don't become a musician. You'll have to be much better than a man to get a job. Do something useful. Be a doctor. Buy yourself a good cello, get together with some colleagues, and have a great time playing chamber music." And in retrospect, he was absolutely right. I was good in sciences, so for three years, I majored in zoology and genetics and sat there with a microscope. But every Thursday and Friday night, I was not allowed to go out on dates because it was chamber-music night in my house. My father would invite friends, my mother would bake her wonderful cakes, and we'd play till all hours. And after three years, I really wanted to play the cello, and this time, it was my decision.

Now, I'm doing exactly what I want to do. I'm a professional cellist in the Winnipeg Symphony, and every Thursday night, my father comes to my house and we play together.

Arlene Dahl, cellist, Winnipeg, Manitoba

Arlene Dahl and her father, Alfred Dahl, Winnipeg, Manitoba

Off and running

To a lot of farmers, land is a third child or a second wife: it feels pretty dear. Yet it isn't a God-given right, and just because your dad was a farmer doesn't mean your land is sacred and no one else can have it. You've got to treat farming as a profession, and if you want to survive, you've got to learn the ropes.

A lot of farmers start farming right out of school, and their only guidance is how their father or neighbour did it, which is advice coming from someone who farmed 40 years ago. Instead, they should look at today's practices and ideas; otherwise, they're never going to catch up. I use computer programs designed for farms: all year long, my records, estimates, pieces of equipment and hours of use of each piece get plugged in and come back to tell me how many bushels of grain I need to break even, and my capital costs and investments are figured into it. It helps me make my decisions.

I appreciate the concerns about the use of chemicals, but I don't subscribe to them. If these products were hazardous and dangerous to use, they would be taken off the market; but people who get sick from herbicides and pesticides probably don't exercise proper precautions, and whose fault is it if they get sick? Every day on the news, there is something that causes cancer, but who is to know? I appreciate the fact that 20 years from now, some of these chemicals may be discovered to cause cancer or lung disease, but I don't want to live in fear of everything.

Would I like my children to be farmers? That's a question everybody asks me. My children do well in school, and if they can guide themselves through high academic achievement, they may find a better profession than farming, because half of it is

Giant straw bales, the Wintering Hills, Alberta

Eve Beierbach and goat on the family ranch, Cypress Hills, Saskatchewan

weather. You can do everything right and end up with nothing, whereas in other fields, right is right. But if you want to excel, you've got to be a step ahead of the pack. So when I'm done farming and I'm a step or two ahead of everyone else, that will be like a kick in the pants for whoever takes the farm over: he should be off and running.

Ian McPhadden, farmer, Milden, Saskatchewan

They won't give it up

After I lived in the East for a good many years, I came back to the prairies. I need that enormous courtesy of people who always seem to recognize a friend and a stranger. There had been the big oil boom and the high agricultural prices, but in the most profound sense, nothing had changed. The prairie—its space, its wind and that enormous sky—does place its print on people. When you return, you have a sense that you're not only going home but that you're again complete. You are part of the rhythm of the prairies.

When my father homesteaded here in 1905, the open plains extended much farther east and north because the fires kept the bush down. There was that perpetual wind, and you heard about people who couldn't endure the prairies and in a tragic number of cases took their own lives or left. And notwithstanding the

enormous amount of intelligently applied hard work, there was, with few exceptions, little prosperity here.

Yet many of the prairie people would do nothing else. Never mind the difficulties. Never mind the wind. Never mind the drought and the grasshoppers. There's a sense of space and freedom, and they won't give it up.

Ralph Hedlin, business consultant, Calgary, Alberta

Wind

When I was a child, we would get these enormous electrical storms during the dry days of summer. Because our window glass wasn't of good quality, we had to get our pillows and press them to the glass to counter the wind. I remember holding those pillows against the windows on the west side of the house when a thunderstorm was coming. The wind would press tightly against the panes, and then, one bang, and it would go through.

Ralph Hedlin, business consultant, Calgary, Alberta

Summer lightning storm at sunset near Brandon, Manitoba

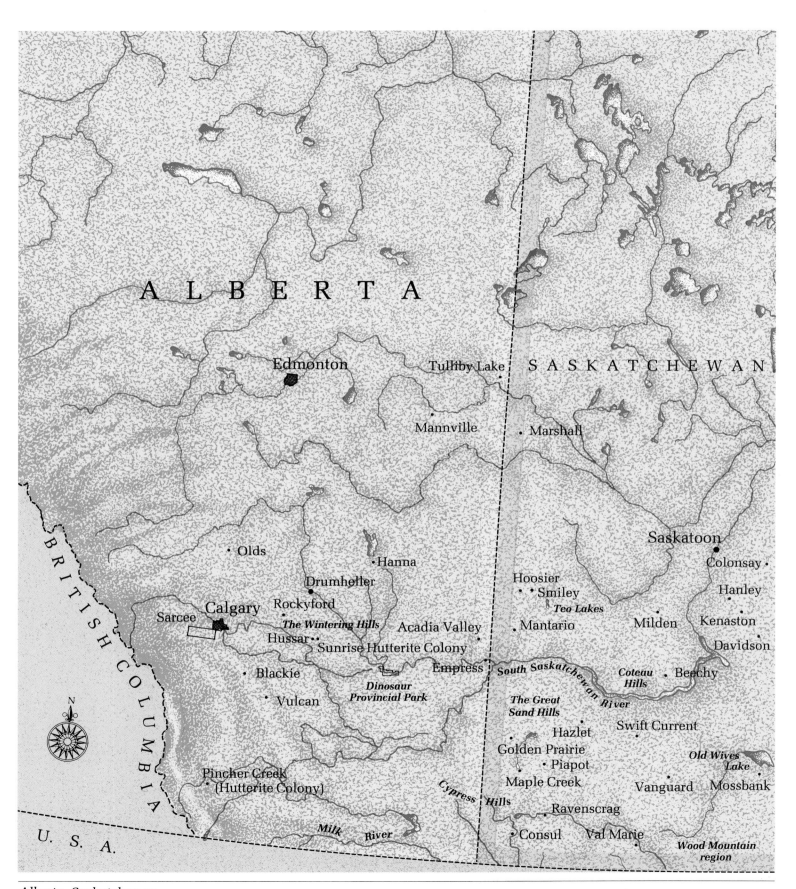

Alberta, Saskatchewan

Saskatchewan and Manitoba with inset of the Prairie Provinces

Story Index